When Evil Came
to Good Hart

Mardi Link

WHEN EVIL CAME
TO GOOD HART

THE UNIVERSITY OF MICHIGAN PRESS
Ann Arbor

2011   2010   2009   2008   4   3   2   1

A CIP catalog record for this book is available from the British Library.

Library of Congress Cataloging-in-Publication Data

Link, Mardi.
    When evil came to Good Hart / Mardi Link.
       p.   cm.
    ISBN-13: 978-0-472-11666-9 (cloth : alk. paper)
    ISBN-10: 0-472-11666-5 (cloth : alk. paper)
    ISBN-13: 978-0-472-03315-7 (pbk. : alk. paper)
    ISBN-10: 0-472-03315-8 (pbk. : alk. paper)
       1. Mass murder—Michigan—Good Hart.   I. Title.
    HV6534.G66L56   2008
    364.152'30977488—dc22   2008015028

Photographs courtesy of Michigan State Police

To my boys

Acknowledgments

I have so much gratitude toward the many people in northern Michigan and elsewhere who welcomed me into their homes, their businesses, their past, and their present. Thanks to book-lover extraordinaire Trina Hayes; mobile tour guide Bill Little; Good Hart historian Carolyn Sutherland and her husband, Jim. Linda Bolton gave me a gracious tour of her home in Good Hart, a beautiful and charming example of Bliss architecture that she and her husband Rick have had lovingly restored by Bill Glass. Bonnie Bliss Weitzel has let nothing destroy her love of Good Hart, and for that she has my respect and admiration. Stephanie Guyor is due much credit by anyone who takes in the lovely St. Ignatius Mission Church in a quiet moment.

Sheriff Pete Wallin and Detective J. L. Sumpter of the Emmet County Sheriff's Office graciously opened up their exhaustive records on the case and provided me with their own personal observations and wisdom, which was invaluable. Thank you to *Petoskey News-Review* editor Kendall Stanley for a well-lit room and a pile of old photographs and faded newspaper clips. Thank you, Shannon Akans and Linda Ortiz of the Michigan State Police, for access to that agency's well-organized, behemoth file on the case. I am proud to be a citizen of a state that has the Michigan State Police looking out for our welfare. Thanks to Scott Libin of the Poynter Institute and John Flesher of the Associated Press for lessons in journalistic ethics; thanks to Rod Doherty for getting me started; Al Koski offered his pointed and motivational remarks.

Thanks also to the University of Michigan Press and Mary Erwin for an institutional and personal commitment to Michigan storytelling; Bear River Writer's Conference and Richard McCann; and Antioch Writers Workshop's Betty Crumrine Creative Nonfiction scholarship program. Your support and kindness continue to be immeasurable. Thanks to Lynne Hugo, writer, teacher, and friend. Thank you, Alex Moore, for canoe floats and literary laments; Deb Schepperly, Aimé Merizon, Mary Ellen Geist, and Emily Meier for your kind editorial encouragement.

Thanks to the Drummond Girls for nurturing my love of the north, thanks to my Link family for time alone on the Lake Huron shore, thanks to my sons Owen, Luke, and Will, three bright, happy, and thriving boys despite their preoccupied mother. And finally, thank you, Pete Morton, for continuing to ask me every writer's favorite question: "What happens next?"

Contents

A Note to Readers   xi

A Stranger Comes to Town   1
Call the Law   4
Will Be Back   10
The Boss   18
The Mentals   27
The Phony   32
Gun Country   39
Following the Money   44
The Tipsters   60
A Leg Man   67
The Alibi   75
Closing In   86
The Case for Prosecution   91
The Leavenworth Letter Theory   101
Another Killing   113
Manhunts in the North Woods   117
The Sleuths   123
The Good People of Good Hart   132
A Bliss House   138
The Literary Ladies of Lamkin   144
A Healing   149
Epilogue: Status of Case No. 7471   154

Who's Who   161
Sources and Resources   165
Further Reading   175

Photographs   *Following page 74*

A Note to Readers

*The true crime empire continues to thrive because modern culture still
offers no systematic and satisfying way to come to terms with human
evil. The question posed here is fundamentally theological: is evil a super-
natural power engaged in a timeless, cosmic struggle against the forces
of Good, or do bad things just happen randomly in an amoral universe
devoid of any larger meaning?*

—Karen Halttunen, *Murder Most Foul: The Killer and the
American Gothic Imagination*

This is a true story. It was written nearly forty years after the murder of the
Robison family, and many of the people you will meet in these pages were
deceased long before I began writing about them. Meticulous records of
the case were kept by both the Michigan State Police and the Emmet
County Sheriff's Office, including taped and written interviews of friends,
family members, business associates, suspects, and others in the midst, and
on the fringes, of the investigation.

In addition, the case was thoroughly covered by reporters working for
the *New York Times,* United Press International, the Associated Press, the
Chicago Tribune, the *Detroit News,* the *Detroit Free Press,* the *Petoskey News-
Review,* the *Traverse City Record Eagle,* the *Harbor Light,* and other newspapers and magazines. Even the noir and titillating *True Detective* magazine
published an in-depth article on the crime, with names disguised. Quoted
material attributed to deceased persons or to persons still living whom I
was unable to interview was obtained from these official reports and journalistic accounts.

Other sources I consulted include Michigan State Attorney General
records, U.S. Army Military Intelligence records, crime scene photographs, investigative photographs, Freedom of Information Act filings,
compilations of local history, personal interviews with year-round and
summer residents of Good Hart, Harbor Springs, Charlevoix, and Petoskey, Michigan, and my own observations. Any errors of omission, history,
fact, or judgment are mine.

A Stranger Comes to Town

Some say that the village of Good Hart, Michigan, is haunted. It is not haunted in the manner that most well-rooted places can become haunted. There is no ghost here that I have seen or felt the opaque presence of, no dark wraith or caped phantom dragging chains in the night or galloping through town on a mist-shrouded mount. No, this diminutive northern coastal town of well-tended cottages, ancient trees, Native American legends, and a clenched fist of locals is haunted by an answer that will not come.

In June 1968, a wealthy Detroit family, the Robisons, was slain here inside their summer cottage by an unknown assailant, who murdered them while they sat at their dining room table playing a game of double solitaire. Today the guilty person is a stranger still, officially at least. Forty years later Good Hart still asks, "Who killed our summer people, and why?"

The Robisons—Richard, Shirley, and their four children—came to Good Hart every summer to "find their bliss," as the saying goes. And from all accounts, for a time they did find it. The family drove the 275 miles north as soon as school let out for the summer, and planned to spend the next three months at Blisswood, a private development of pine log and birch bark summer homes nestled in the protective dunes alongside Lake Michigan. Like countless other downstate families, the Robisons left behind the schedule of the city, replaced its grime with beach sand and its grit with carefree hunts for Petoskey stones. Every June, when they drove away from their home in a suburb of Detroit and headed north, they also left behind the crime of the city—or so they thought.

Today, fewer than five hundred people live in Good Hart year-round; most have grown weary of the endless questions about the Robisons that visitors bring with them. A brutal, unsolved murder is not what anyone would want his or her village to be known for, especially a village that owes its livelihood to the hospitality it gives to strangers. If locals do talk, the one Robison they talk about first is Susie. She was Richard and Shirley's youngest child and only daughter—just seven years old when she was murdered.

That is the same age I was in July 1968, when I too traveled north with my parents and my brother, to visit for the first time what became our family's summer cottage. Though my own grandfather built the cottage and named it Bob-O-Link, he had not built it for my grandmother or for his own children, but for his sister, Meta.

My great-aunt was a private woman, nervous around groups larger than two or three, even if they were members of her own family. I think of her now as an odd woman—tiny, thin, proper, and tense, with the curious fate of being part of a jovial German family that liked to eat and drink and laugh and play endless games of cards. It was no wonder, then, that we had never been invited to her cottage, but on July 22, 1968, we were on our way north for a camping trip. Our route would take us within a half mile of Bob-O-Link, and we would be stopping by for the afternoon. I have a feeling that my father may have announced our visit to Meta, politely of course, rather than asking. Back then, my family and I were the strangers coming to town.

It was one of a handful of clear-sunshine days that arrive in northern Michigan every July, and I was wearing my bathing suit under my clothes as we headed north. Though I had never been to Bob-O-Link, the beach was already the stuff of Link family legend. Sand, white and fine-grained as icing sugar, squeaked under your bare feet when you walked. Water so clear you could watch schools of minnows swirl around your legs. Pine trees with giant cones, snake grass that you could break apart at each black-ringed segment then snap back together again, lowland pools of tadpoles and tiny toads. What more could a young girl on summer vacation possibly desire?

In the backseat of our black Ford Galaxy I could hear the familiar voice of Ernie Harwell on the radio, for my father was listening to a Tigers game on WJR. Next to him, my mother was going over the menu she had planned for our weeklong camping trip. Without warning, there was a break in Ernie's commentary, and the car radio crackled out news of the wicked crime. A father, a mother, three sons, and one daughter. All dead. All killed with guns, the newsman said. There was more to the report: the girl, the daughter, the sister, was seven years old. The same age as me. My dad turned off the radio, and it grew quiet inside our car. How does a seven-year-old girl come to understand that evil exists in this world? How does a whole town come to understand it?

* * *

In the summer of 2007 I visited Good Hart for the first time. By then I had been following the unsolved murders of the Robison family, unofficially and irregularly, for almost four decades. In my teens, I occasionally saw Susie in my dreams. In college, I looked up articles about the crime in *Reader's Index*. In my first job as a newspaper reporter, I learned how to read police reports and wondered about the details in the report on the Robisons.

On that first visit to Good Hart, a friend of a friend introduced me to Carolyn Sutherland, the owner of the town's oldest business, the Good Hart General Store. She was short, petite, sun-tanned already in May, with cropped hair that dared you to comment on its orangeness. And she was glowering at me through her firmly closed front screen door.

"This is my friend," the woman I'd just met said, by way of introduction. "She's a writer and she's working on a book about Good Hart."

"A writer, huh?" Carolyn crossed her arms over her chest. "Well, can you spell 'Get lost'?"

"My computer has spell check for that," I fired back.

She squinted back at me, arms crossed and leaning forward, showing no signs of easing up on the door. But she said, "Well, if you're a friend of Jeanne's, I guess you can't be all bad."

"Um, to tell you the truth, I really only met her five minutes ago."

Beside me, Jeanne Moore, the friend of a friend who was doing me a favor, cringed.

Then from behind the screen, a grin. The door swung open wide.

"All right, you'd better come in. Before people around here start filling your head with all sorts of crazy stuff."

And for the next year, people around there did fill my head with crazy stuff. With their stories of compassion and tragedy, resourcefulness and craftsmanship, beauty and ugliness.

Welcome, dear reader, to Good Hart.

July 22, 1968

We don't know *anything*. We don't know
how it was done . . . why it was done
. . . or for sure exactly when it was
done. And we certainly don't know who
did it. All we know is, it was done.

— Wayne Richard Smith, Emmet County prosecutor,
July 27, 1968

When asked to explain, Monnie Bliss told his parents, his neighbors, the police, and anyone else who would listen that he just thought a coon had died, that was all. A fat old coon had got itself hit by a car or bit by a dog and crawled underneath the fieldstone foundation of the Robison cottage and died. What else could account for that smell? What else, when the wind was blowing off the water just right, could remind the ladies playing bridge next door of picnic meat forgotten too long in the sun?

Though Monnie's cursory walk around the outside of the Robisons' found no sign of any such doomed critter, it was a plausible explanation. Blisswood, the bluff of summer cottages Monnie and his father, Chauncey Bliss, built alongside the shore of Lake Michigan is a pine log and elm bark outpost surrounded by hardwood forest so dense that, even today, if you walk a quarter mile in at noon on a sunny day you'll have a hard time reading the finer details on a topographical map. In 1968, deer, bear, beaver, bobcat, opossum, porcupine, and raccoons still reigned, far outnumbering both the area's locals and their summer people.

The hostess of the next-door bridge party, Gladys Moore, was not pleased by the odor. She and her husband, Russell, had made the annual trip up to Good Hart from their home in Coldwater earlier than usual this year to get their cottage spic-and-span for Gladys's three-day "hen party," as the men called it. She and her lady friends would play bridge, snack, yak, and enjoy the fresh July air. And now some dead animal was making that impossible. Days ago she had complained to Monnie's father Chauncey about the smell, now all five of her friends had left because they couldn't

4

bear it, and the odor was getting worse. She'd just have to talk with the senior Mr. Bliss again. After all, he and his son and their Krude Kraft Construction Company had built most of the cottages in the area and continued to make a nice bit of pocket money by handling the upkeep on them. You expected better upkeep than this.

"We had the card table outside, it was so hot," Gladys would later say to police. "When the wind changed to the north, the stench was so bad we could hardly stand it. First, our place gets broken into for a sex party and now this."

Chauncey, eighty-four, was known to forget things here and there, but he recalled that the Moore's place did get broken into sometime that spring. Nothing was stolen or broken, but the beds had been used. And Gladys was right about the stench. He'd been over there to water the flowers while the Robisons were away on their big trip and he'd smelled it himself. Monnie would just have to go back and get to the bottom of it.

* * *

Well, it was just plain odd. There was no logical explanation for such a thing. The leather strap that lifted the metal bar latching the front door of the Robison place was pulled to the inside. There would be no easy way to open it then, unless you were inside, too. Monnie and his new carpenter's helper, a local Odawa Indian man by the name of Steve Shananaquet, tried to look through the front window, but a heavy drape was pulled all the way shut, blocking their view. A quick walk around back found the lakeside door padlocked. They would need hand tools if they were going to get inside the place. "Get me a flat bar and that file from my truck," Monnie told Steve.

With the tools he set to work. Monnie pried the wooden door molding out with the flat bar just far enough to slip the file under the black latch, raise it up off its iron tooth, and pull the door open. Steve stood close behind, looking over his boss' shoulder at the indecent scene inside.

Flies. And someone's legs. They were the bare legs of a woman, and they were protruding from underneath a blanket, one foot still wearing a beige high heel. A dark lump—a torso?—in a hallway beyond. Everywhere a bluish haze of air not breathed for must have been a month, at least. And that smell. Both men brought their calloused hands to their faces.

"What . . . what do we . . . do?" Monnie asked. It was less a question, maybe, than a way to end this moment, like waking up from a panicked dream. If he could speak, he must be awake. But if he could speak, this must be real.

"Call 'em," said Steve. "Call the law."

* * *

Undersheriff Clifford Fosmore was the top lawman in Emmet County, for this one week anyway. His boss, Sheriff Richard Zink, had taken his young family on a camping vacation to Yellowstone National Park, and in his absence Fosmore was in charge. The deer and birds and such common up north might be interesting to people from downstate, but Zink and his family were going to see coyotes, wolves, and maybe even a mountain lion or a grizzly. As of 3:00 p.m. on Monday, July 22, Fosmore didn't need to fantasize about his boss catching sight of a big-game predator; he was about to begin tracking a predator of his own.

"There's a body inside one of our cottages," Monnie said to the deputy who answered the phone at the Sheriff's office. "And it's been laying there awhile. There might be some others."

The Bliss name was recognized and given some credence at the sheriff's office. They were one of the area's pioneer families, here since the end of the Civil War, fruit farmers turned developers. Monnie Bliss had even been supervisor of Readmond Township and was lawfully deputized. This, they knew at the outset, was no crank call. The deputy told Monnie to hold tight and stay at the scene, he'd radio Fosmore and they'd be on their way shortly. Monnie agreed to meet them out on the road and direct the men down the bluff to the hidden cottage below. Even though it was part of the sheriff's duty to patrol the Good Hart area, the cottage was so remote that the lawmen needed a guide to the scene.

* * *

Murder was not a crime anyone from Emmet County was accustomed to, including those who worked in the Sheriff's Office. It's as true now as it was then. The deputies are more likely to investigate a stolen canoe, late night hi-jinks at one of the area's golf courses, or teenagers at a beer bash in the woods. Domestic calls, drunk and disorderly, and drug deals are the most dangerous things they encounter with any regularity. When Monnie said the word "body" into the phone, it must have been nothing short of shocking. The last homicide in the department's files happened a full decade earlier, when city police in Petoskey had gone to the home of a local man to ask him about his odd behavior in town that day, and he showed them the body of his dead mother, rolled up in a carpet. Monnie had served on the jury that convicted him.

The deputy headed out in a patrol car for the half-hour drive north to Good Hart and picked up Undersheriff Fosmore on the way. While they were en route, word spread over the police radio and, just as efficiently, via party line gossip. Soon three more sheriff's deputies, the county prosecutor, the Mackinaw City police chief, a reporter for the local newspaper, a Petoskey city patrolman, and a local parole officer were following closely behind. Altogether, ten capable men were on their way to Blisswood, most born and raised within thirty miles of the crime scene, sharing a century's worth of protect-and-serve experience among them. It would not be enough.

On their approach, the men could see that someone had propped the cottage's door open with an iron horseshoe stake. While Monnie waited in the yard, Fosmore and his crew entered to the dark buzzing of a thousand flies, the sporadic ring of a telephone and, despite the afternoon heat, the sound of a furnace clicking off and then back on again. Someone's flashlight cut the men's path through the daytime dark. The newspaper reporter had thought to bring his camera along and its repeated flashes illuminated the scene in bursts.

To the left of the doorway, lying on her stomach, lay a grown woman. A red plaid blanket covered all but her legs. Underneath, her lime-colored dress was pulled up to her waist, her underclothes rolled down to her ankles. The men walked on. In the hallway, three more bodies. A man, a boy, and a young girl, piled one on top of another. In the doorway to a back bedroom, a teenager, crumpled on the floor, a few playing cards held in his hand, a few more scattered on the floor nearby. Inside the bedroom, another teenager lying flat, his arms stretched above his head as if reaching for something or someone.

Back in the center room, an object on the floor caught Undersheriff Fosmore's attention. He found a paper towel in the kitchen, picked the object up with it, and headed for an outside door. Any outside door.

In the daylight he held up his prize—a bloody claw hammer—and the reporter snapped a photo. Officers opened two crank-out windows and broke the glass out of four more with a piece of metal pipe. Back outside, fresh air, sunlight, a light breeze in the tops of the oak and pine. Someone noticed a note taped to one of the glass panes in one of the side windows flanking the front door. In their hurry to get inside the cottage, they had each missed it. Scrawled on a piece of paper towel were the words, "Will be back 7–10. Robison." Beside the note, a crack in the glass and bullet holes.

Inside, Fosmore had counted six bodies. He said the number out loud now. The other men agreed. Yes, there were six. That was everyone then, Monnie told them. Good Christ, the whole family.

Slain were Richard Robison, forty-two, Shirley Robison, forty, Ritchie Robison, nineteen, Gary Robison, seventeen, Randy Robison, twelve, and Susie Robison, seven. A well-to-do Lutheran family from Lathrup Village, a suburb of Detroit. Summering in Good Hart for a few precious weeks at a time for the past twelve years. This was to be the first time the family was going to spend the whole summer up north at the cottage they had named Summerset. A reward for the success Richard had made of his advertising and publishing business.

Monnie estimated the Robisons arrived in town on June 16, a few days after the kids' school let out. It was to be a whole easy summer of building sand castles and painting the landscape with watercolors, of late morning pancake breakfasts and evening campfires on the beach. The teenaged boys complained of spending the whole summer away from their friends, but they'd meet new friends up here, and they'd adjust. They'd collect Petoskey stones, catch Monarch butterflies, and roast marshmallows. It was a simple but enduring dream, shared by thousands of Michigan families, but one that for the Robisons this summer in 1968, lasted just eight days.

* * *

Though Readmond Township had an operating post office as early as December 1874, the official incorporation of the village of Good Hart itself, as far as duly recorded legal deeds are concerned, started in 1910 when Mitchell Assinaway, an Odawa Indian and widower, sold the property the town now rests on to Ivan Swift, pioneer, farmer, artist, and sometime poet, for one dollar and "other valuable considerations." What those other considerations were remain a mystery, though a reader can get a good idea of the land's natural blessings from two stanzas of one of Ivan's poems titled "Landing."

These trees and plants—birch, hemlock and pine,
Dogwood and bittersweet—
Are of the soil that is my soil.
This breeze is our breath,
This lake and fog and sun
Our common nourishment.

Let those who will, burn the paved hills
And fragment the sky on iron wings!
They describe circles, large or small —
And will make landing here —
Where we cultivate in peace
And wait in silent praise.

A year earlier, in 1909, the *Petoskey News* correspondent for Good Hart welcomed the long-awaited arrival of June and its accompanying promise of good weather with a burst of equally inspired expression: "Dame Nature is surely doing her part toward making this world a thing of beauty and a joy forever. With the forest in full foliage and the abundance of blossoms on fruit trees and wild cherries, etc, it is a grand sight to feast one's eyes upon."

Good Hart had a long and proud history before Assinaway deeded his property to Swift. An ancient history, though events hadn't been written down because the area was primarily an Odawa Indian village. Much of this history was commonplace and domestic, but much of it was eerie and filled with legend and mystery. The area was named L'Arbre Croche, in French meaning "Place of the Crooked Tree." There are two famous trees in the area, the Crooked Tree, which is thought to have once been firmly rooted in the bluff just north of Good Hart and was so large and distinctive that it functioned as a kind of marker for visitors to the area traveling by water. The other was the Council Tree that grew for centuries a few miles further north and provided the shade where Menominees, Chippewas, and Odawas met to discuss the aftermath of the 1763 massacre at Fort Michilimackinac.

In 1955 Chauncey Bliss, Monnie's father, erected wooden signs that mark the places of each of these legends, as well as Middle Village, St. Ignatius Church, and Devil's Elbow so motorists on holiday could learn more about the area. Newer versions of the original signs remain posted along Lake Shore Drive between Harbor Springs and Cross Village today.

Devil's Elbow is a hairpin curve on M-119 that horseshoes around a deep gulley where, according to legend, the devil scooped out a giant hollow of ground after the local Odawas were ravaged by a plague, probably smallpox. British soldiers were killed here, too, and it could have been their souls the devil was grabbing for. The sign for this point of historical interest reads, "A flowing spring in this ravine was believed by Indian tribes to be the home of an evil spirit who haunted the locality during the hours of darkness."

July 23, 1968

It is noted that a window on the
east side has three holes in one of
the panes. They are of the type that
is made by a bullet. A piece of paper
is fixed to the glass with tape. In
the center of this paper the following
is printed in ink, "WILL BE BACK,
signed ROBISON."

— Michigan State Police trooper Edward Hancock's
police report, filed July 22, 1968

For a month the bodies of the Robison family had lain where their killer had left them. A month of July sunshine, a month of radiant heat from a gas furnace, a month of closed windows and closed drapes, a month of carpenter ants, millipedes, microscopic fungi, sow bugs, and maggots. From the maggots came the flies. Tens of thousands of flies.

"The visible interior floor is covered with dead flies, live flies are en masse," Trooper Edward Hancock wrote. Such was the state of the aged and macabre crime scene he and his fellow Michigan State Police officers found when they arrived, via desperate invitation from the undersheriff, at the Robison cottage.

It was past afternoon and getting on into evening by the time Col. John Lewinski and Trooper Hancock initiated their solemn work. They noted two late-model but pollen-covered cars, a Ford and a Chrysler, parked in the cottage's driveway. A pole lamp in the yard was lighted, casting a weakened glow on the oak trees, though there were no lights turned on inside the place. Both doors of the cottage were propped open and there were several broken windows, but the smell emanating from inside was still sickening. There was a retching sweetness to it, and the sticky scent hung in the air like rotting honeysuckle. Covering their mouths with white handkerchiefs, the troopers entered the log-walled twilight to catalog the human damage within.

The first body they documented was the mother's—Shirley. Near the door and lying face down in the living room, she had on only one shoe, a plain beige high-heeled pump. The other was on a chair nearby, as if it had been tossed there haphazardly. Her legs were spread, toes pointed toward one another, a pair of white panties and a white girdle, cut in two by something jagged, still around her left ankle. A plaid camp blanket, neatly placed almost as if for an indoor picnic, covered her head and back. Underneath, her knit dress and her slip were yanked up to her waist, leaving her exposed. It would take the lab specialists to make it official, but the officers thought that Shirley had probably been raped.

In the hallway, a pyramid of bodies. The father, Richard, was lying on his stomach, his cheek pressed onto a furnace register. Face down on top of his father was Randall, the youngest of the three sons, his legs resting on his father's shoulders. Wedged in the narrow bit of space between the wall and Randall was Susie, the baby of the family and only daughter. When she was born, the Robisons must have sighed happily. Finally, a girl.

Ahead, a tall teenager lying on his stomach, arms twisted awkwardly, his body lying half in the hallway and half inside one of the back bedrooms. This was the oldest son, Richard Jr.—the one enrolled in college, the one who was supposed to be the heir to his father's success.

Further inside the same bedroom, lying on his back, his right arm extended out as if to grab something just beyond his reach, his suit jacket bunched up around his shoulders, was another teenager, Gary. A smaller, younger physical copy of his older brother.

The troopers carefully stepped around pools of dried blood on the floor, taking note of bloody drag marks and bloody footprints. In the corner of the living room there was a table covered with a deck of playing cards in disarray, a game of chance abruptly interrupted. The troopers' final glance before exiting the scene to guard it for their science-minded colleagues would have registered ordinary things: camera bags, an open suitcase, three dressy coats—a man's, a woman's, and a little girl's—spread neatly over the back of the couch.

By 6:15 p.m. the medical examiner arrived from Petoskey. Dr. Richard Weber went inside to see to the dead, while troopers Lewinski and Hancock, outside now, pulled out their pens and notebooks and changed their focus to the living.

Monnie Bliss was still at the scene, and they started their interviews with him. Just a few questions, they said, to get a better idea of what had happened and when. Not an interrogation, nothing like that, just a friendly discussion.

How had the bodies been there for a month without being discovered? Hadn't he noticed the smell? Of course he had noticed it, Monnie said, but it could have been spoiled food in the refrigerator, it could have been a dead animal trapped in the crawl space. When he came to investigate, he'd even brought along a shovel and a cardboard box in case he had to dispose of some rotted thing. He never imagined it was anything like this, he told the troopers. Never anything at all like this.

And the last time he'd seen the Robisons? Late June, the twenty-fourth. Monnie remembered the exact date because it was just one day after his own teenaged son, Norman, had died, killed up the road in a motorbike accident. Monnie, along with his wife, found that body, too. The day before the funeral Richard Robison, "Dick" to those who knew him, had stopped by to offer his condolences, gave the Blisses twenty dollars toward the cost of flowers for the funeral, and apologized for not being able to attend. Dick said that the whole Robison family was leaving on a trip the next day, and he gave Monnie his cottage keys, in case the caretaker needed to get inside while they were away, in case anything went wrong. All the summer people depended on him for things like that.

During the past month then, when the family was supposed to be out of town, didn't Monnie find it odd that there were two brand-new and rather expensive-looking cars parked in the Robisons' driveway? No, Monnie said, because the Robisons owned a small airplane that Dick knew how to fly, and that the family used for both business and pleasure travel. Plus, they could have been picked up by someone else, a friend maybe, and driven to the airport. If that were the case, he said, they wouldn't have needed either car.

If Monnie had the door key, why had it been so difficult to get inside the cottage? Why did he have to crack the doorframe? Monnie explained the workings of the unusual wrought iron door locks he made by hand in his metal shop and installed on all of the cottages he built. His father came up with the original design, and these locks looked more appropriate with the decor of the rustic cottages than a standard doorknob would.

The hand-forged Bliss-designed locks have an iron bar on the inside of the door. A leather rawhide string is attached to the bar and works as a lever to move the bar in and out of an iron notch. The rawhide is to be pulled through a hole in the door to the outside when the owners leave. If someone is in the cottage and pulls the rawhide string all the way to the inside, the doors cannot be opened from the outside. The Robison cottage, Summerset, had such a lock, and oddly, the string was pulled to the inside when Monnie first checked on the place, though of course no one answered his knock.

Monnie could offer nothing further, and so troopers sent him home and went looking for his father, Chauncey Bliss. Hancock and Lewinski interviewed Chauncey and his wife, May, at 9:00 p.m. up on the bluff near their house, which overlooked the crime scene. The Robisons had been up from downstate for a week or so before stopping by to tell him they were leaving for a trip to Kentucky, then Florida. Yes, he saw the two cars in the driveway and yes, he even saw the bullet holes in the window, but he just hadn't gotten around to replacing the glass. He had no idea the family had been murdered; he thought some local troublemakers shot out the glass with pellet guns.

"They told how he had built the cottages in this area and how he had sold the land on which the cottages are built," Trooper Hancock wrote. "We came up here to get away from this kind of thing," the senior Bliss would later tell a reporter.

From there, troopers interviewed two other summer people, Richard Nordstrom of Birmingham and Gladys Moore, whose complaints to Monnie had led to the discovery of the crime. Nordstrom showed up near the crime scene, was acting frantic, carrying a cocktail of some kind of clear liquor, speed-talking about his friendship with Dick and the times they enjoyed a cup of coffee together in Dick's Southfield office. Talk to a guy named Joe Scolaro, Nordstrom told the troopers. He worked for Dick in his advertising business and always knew Dick's every move.

In her cottage next door, Gladys Moore told the troopers that she knew something had to be wrong because of that horrible smell. It had absolutely ruined her annual ladies bridge party, the one she looked forward to all year. Her idea of danger in the area was a propane gas leak, not a murderer on the loose. She and her husband had been thinking about selling their place and leaving the area completely—this made that decision a lot easier.

By now, it was getting dark outside, and the two troopers returned to the cottage and guarded the crime scene against any further contamination. Their colleagues from the mobile crime lab were on their way from state police headquarters in East Lansing, some four hours south, but still several miles out. Their police radios didn't work in this desolate location behind the coastal dunes, and so they could do little but wait. The crowd of curious onlookers that had gathered at the site throughout the day had drifted away, and the two troopers and two sheriff's deputies were the only people left.

From inside the cottage the men could hear the periodic ringing of the family's telephone, and as the sun sunk below the Lake Michigan horizon they were left to wonder who was on the other end of the line. A family member perhaps, or a friend. The killer even, calling out of some sadistic sense of curiosity.

It was then that one of the men noticed wisps of smoke rising out of the cottage's open windows and doors. Small puffs at first, then great black plumes. They thought the place was on fire and rushed inside to investigate. What they found was more repulsive even than the smell that still infused the air for a hundred yards in every direction. So repulsive in fact, that trooper Hancock felt compelled to document it in his report: "[T]he smoke was caused by the furnace, a floor hung type, that was under some of the bodies in the hallway. Particles of flesh and such were falling on the furnace and causing it to smoke."

When the troopers from East Lansing drove their mobile crime lab into the driveway, it didn't take them long to realize that they had an old crime scene, and it was in quickly disintegrating pieces. These were the men who could make sense of the senseless, who could make the illogical, logical again. They could catalog, preserve, collect, identify, and even, if there was enough to work with, understand. These were the men who could re-create the frightening drama of this murder and document a beginning, a middle, and an end.

Troopers Herb Olney, Hugh Fish, and David Larsen pulled on gas masks and went inside. They started with the easiest items to remove from the scene, the Robison family's expensive camera equipment, and then turned their attention to the spent ammunition.

The three men found four and a half boxes of .22-caliber rifle cartridges, which turned out to belong to the Robisons for use in their Mossberg rifle, but they also found four fired .25-caliber bullets and eleven spent .22-caliber shell casings that didn't belong to the Mossberg. These fifteen rounds had, in fact, put the holes in the outside window, but also tore through a yellow upholstered chair, lodged in a braided floor rug, cracked a record album, and splintered the wood floor. The bullets were most likely fired from a handgun. The shell casings were from a rifle.

At least two weapons, then, had been used in the crime. This meant that there were either two shooters, or just one with two weapons. Officers couldn't find either gun, not inside the cottage nor anywhere outside on the grounds in the surrounding area.

The men worked through the night examining the scene, making diagrams, dusting for fingerprints and handprints and collecting evidence while Hancock and Lewinski continued to stand guard outside. By 10:30 the next morning, they had done all they could do and released the bodies of the six members of the Robison family into the care of the medical examiner, Dr. Richard Weber.

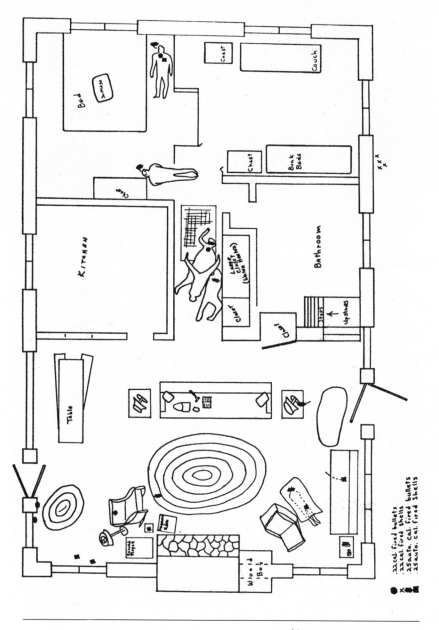

Michigan State
Police rendering
of the crime
scene sketched
the day after
the bodies were
found

Emmet County had no morgue in 1968, so Dr. Weber's plan was to conduct the autopsies in the same place he always did, Little Traverse Hospital in Petoskey, the nearest medical facility. But when the caravan of Weber, his staff, funeral personnel, law enforcement officers, and miscellaneous curious hangers-on arrived there with the victims, they were refused entry. The bodies of the family were in too degraded a state to be allowed into a hospital, and so after a brief discussion the grim procession traveled on through town to the Emmet County Fairgrounds.

There the men assembled a makeshift morgue in a chicken coop, and Dr. Weber, assisted by pathologist Dr. Jean Webster, worked hurriedly for four hours and twenty minutes on the six autopsies while five state troopers looked on. Cause of death for each member of the family was ruled to be gunshot wounds to the head, though Susie had also been struck in the head with a blunt object—probably a carpenter's hammer, Dr. Weber noted, because of her crescent-shaped wound. The few valuables found on the bodies were turned over to Trooper Fish of the state police.

Shirley was the first Robison to receive the medical examiner's attention. On her ruined finger was a 14-karat gold wedding band with the sentiment "Richard to Shirley 9-27-47" engraved on the inside. Her silver Hamilton wristwatch had stopped at 6:40. Missing was her three-and-a-quarter carat diamond ring. It had been on her finger when she left for the cottage, her mother Aileen Fulton was certain, because she had pleaded with her daughter to take it off and store it in the family's safe deposit box while they were away. Shirley declined, telling her mother that the ring was fully insured and she would never, ever take it off her finger.

"That don't make any difference! It's your life can go with that because they're robbing people for less than that," Aileen said.

Shirley's husband, Richard, was next. His seventeen-jewel Chrometer had stopped at 9:59, and his wedding band matched his wife's—"Shirley to Richard 9-27-47." The previous year the couple had celebrated their twentieth anniversary. Richard also had a Mason's ring on his right hand and a St. Christopher's medal around his neck.

Then, the boys. Timex watches, white handkerchiefs and black plastic combs slid into trouser pockets for each son and black leather wallets with new ten-dollar bills inside.

And finally, Susie. Her only remaining possession the pair of pink plastic pigtail holders in her hair.

If anyone thought it strange that the last few mysteries the Robison family had to offer were searched out in the same place that prizewinning poultry was judged every August, they kept those thoughts to themselves.

That an area veterinarian from Jensen's Animal Hospital in Petoskey made available his x-ray equipment for their grisly task raised no eyebrows, either. The events of the past two days had been beyond strange—they had been sickening and evil, and these crude autopsies were just a very small part of it. The more serious matter was that while the bodies of the destroyed Robison family lay here at the fairgrounds, the person or persons responsible were still out there, the motive unknown.

As the autopsies were being completed, troopers Herb Olney and Hugh Fish discussed how the crime could have been carried out. Someone had staked out a spot in the woods a short distance from the Robison cottage and shot at the family through a window with the rifle, causing an unimaginable panic inside. The killer or killers could have then entered the cottage brandishing the handgun.

Summerset's front and back doors showed no signs of forced entry beyond Monnie's pry-bar marks. Perhaps the family knew their killer. Perhaps they even opened the door to him, hoping for help but instead welcoming their own destruction inside.

Whether stranger, hired gun, familiar face, or random maniac, if the crime happened this way it was an icy heart that stilled itself outside the cottage, there in the woods just north of Good Hart. It might have been a humid day in June, but a frozen heart beat inside whoever watched that privileged summer scene through the cottage window, took skillful aim with hands steady enough to tightly space three rounds, and pulled the trigger.

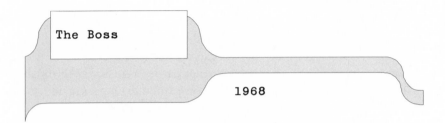

1968

He was kind of a Jekyll and Hyde type.

—Reverend Harvey Peters

No one, police decided, would murder the whole Robison family over something one of the kids did. Or over some domestic transgression of Shirley's. Within days after the crime was discovered, two seasoned detectives from the Michigan State Police were assigned to the case; Detective Lloyd Stearns and Detective John Flis. The rest of their caseload was divvied up among other officers, and their sole concern became finding the killer of the Robisons.

After an early look at the available evidence and collating their initial interviews with the Robisons' family, friends, and Good Hart neighbors, the detectives determined that the chronology of the crime had progressed like this:

June 16. The family travels, in two cars, from their home in Lathrup Village to their cottage in Good Hart.

June 23. Shirley Robison's mother, Aileen Fulton, calls the cottage, speaks with Shirley, and is told that the family is having a good time. No mention is made of a trip.

June 24. The family goes shopping in downtown Petoskey in the morning, returns to their cottage, and is told by neighbors that Monnie Bliss's son, Norman, was killed the night before in a motorbike accident. Dick visits with Norman's grandparents Chauncey and May Bliss and offers his condolences and $20 for funeral flowers. He tells the Bliss family that he will not be able to attend Norman's funeral because the family is leaving the next day for Kentucky and Florida. They'll be gone for two to three weeks.

June 25. Tree trimmer Russell Figg and his teenage helper arrive outside the Robison cottage at 9:30 a.m. to begin precontracted work. Dick tells Figg that the family is awaiting a long distance phone call confirming that their plane is ready to take them on their trip. They

will be leaving either later today or tomorrow. At 10:00 a.m. and
again at 10:30 a.m. Dick calls his banker at the National Bank of Detroit to discuss finances. Figg sees most of the family members
throughout the day. He completes work at 4:30 p.m., and Dick pays
him with a $170 check. At 8:00 or 9:00 p.m. neighbors report hear-
ing gunshots.

June 26. Figg returns to complete his work and remains in the area until
5:00 p.m. but sees no one home at the cottage.

Stearns and Flis speculated that the murders were either a meaningless
rampage by a crazed killer or that the initial target of the murderer was
Dick Robison, with the others tragic collateral damage. If it was Dick, the
detectives were determined to find out why he was targeted. What set of
circumstances had placed him in front of a gunman or gunmen hiding out
in the woods? Something had infuriated, panicked, or alienated this anonymous shooter or shooters enough that, according to the autopsy report,
two rounds were fired into Dick's head and one into his chest. When they
found out the why they might also find out the who, and so Stearns and Flis
started to untangle the knotted strands in the intricate life of Dick Carl
Robison.

Dick had earned his family's upper class lifestyle through hard work.
More than a decade earlier, he had founded R. C. Robison and Associates,
the detectives learned. The company formulated advertising campaigns for
successful Detroit-area businesses and even decided in which outlets the
ads would be run and for how long. Dick also published an arts magazine,
Impresario, that detailed the cultural scene in Detroit and beyond.

"It doesn't look like he had a single enemy," Stearns said when the
crime was still fresh. "We just can't get a handle on this guy."

It would certainly be understandable if Stearns later on regretted making that comment. Dick had enemies, and Stearns and his fellow state
troopers, as well as a whole lineup of Emmet County sheriff's detectives,
would eventually track down and question them.

Yet on the surface and at the beginning of the investigation, Dick Robison looked pretty clean—a devout Lutheran, a strict father, an attentive
husband. He painted watercolors and supported the civic opera. How
many enemies could a man like that really have? Robison's kind of clean
turned out to be not the squeaky kind, but the slippery.

Dick, the detectives soon learned, was a man who inspired corruption
and loyalty in almost equal measure in the men he worked and socialized
with. He was a human enigma, one man with his family, another with his

business associates, and still another when he was alone and looking at the world through his artist's eyes. The detectives knew full well that most people behave differently in different situations, of course, but as they researched Dick's background, detectives found not just shades of the same man, reasonably adjusting to whatever circumstances he encountered, but three totally different men.

Here was a man who knew how to stand at an artist's easel and hold a camel's hair paintbrush. Who knew how to say "No" to his children without regret or second-guessing. Who carried himself as if he was born in his three-piece suit, and who wore all of his clothes neatly starched and pressed, even when on vacation at his summer cottage.

Dick didn't smoke cigarettes and he didn't have a thirst for liquor. He didn't gamble and he didn't care for guns. What he did like was art and money and the prestige they brought him. From his actions and from the opinions the detectives coaxed out of those willing to talk, they learned that Dick wanted as much of both art and money as he could get, and woe to anyone who stood in his way.

"He was either a person that liked you and would do anything for you or a person that didn't and would do anything against you," was one former employee's characterization. The employee's name was Richard Stockwell, and he had quit working for Dick Robison because he didn't like being bullied. A year later, Dick wooed him back with a lucrative salary offer and promises of good behavior. After a week on the job, Dick called him into his office and summarily fired him. "Nobody quits Dick Robison," he told the stunned Stockwell. "Nobody."

Others acquainted with Dick told detectives he was a "tyrant," a "schizophrenic," acted "paranoid and secretive," and held "dogmatic" opinions. Then again, he was "brilliant," "a genius," with a "magnetic" personality and a "sincere" religious faith. Sometimes these conflicting appraisals were volunteered by the same person.

He was a secretive man, but on the last day of his life Dick still left enough of a trail for detectives to follow, and they were reasonably sure that he and his family were, as Monnie had said, preparing to leave on a lengthy trip when they were killed. It was to be a venture in buying real estate, the police learned from interviewing family and friends, with the family traveling via a private jet that would take the six of them to Lexington, Kentucky, and Naples, Florida. Shirley had told her best friend and neighbor, Margaret Smith, and Dick had told his father, Ross Robison, that a man would be coming to stay with them in Good Hart for a few days and then the family and this man would make the trip south together. Margaret told detectives that she phoned Shirley in mid-June, right before the family left for Summerset, to wish her a good trip. Shirley told Margaret that she was worried that everything at the cottage wouldn't be presentable for their guest.

Her fears were eased slightly when Dick called her from the road during one of his many business trips and said their future visitor wanted to talk with her directly. He put the man on the line. "Don't make any fuss, I'm just coming up to relax," the man told her. "Maybe you could make me some of the pasties Dick tells me is a local specialty up there."

Margaret Smith couldn't remember the man's name, but Dick's father did. It was unusual—"Roebert"—and it was his private jet that would bear the family south. Dick's right-hand man at the office, a young guy by the name of Joe Scolaro, would know of the rendezvous as well, Margaret Smith said. A few scant details at least, even if he didn't know everything.

When detectives talked to Joe for the first time, scant details were indeed all he knew about the trip, though he had been left in charge of Robison's business while Dick was away.

"Some man by the name of Mr. Roberts was supposed to go up there and visit them," Joe told Detective Stearns.

"Who is Mr. Roberts?" Stearns asked.

"Beats the hell out of me," Joe said. "Dick used the name a couple of times and then would say, 'Forget it.' Roberts might be . . . a fictitious name, I really don't know. He never linked it directly with anything and when I would ask him who the man was, he wouldn't tell me."

Were Roebert and Mr. Roberts the same man? Was he a business associate of Dick's? Could he be the killer? The detectives didn't know, but continued their search for answers.

They grilled another of Dick's business associates, Walter Muellenhagen. "This is the thing the police were so insistent I ought to know. Who he is and they kept coming back to the same question," Muellenhagen told a reporter. "They would come in here a couple times a week, drop by unexpectedly, call up, anything, and they'd stop by and they'd always bring up this question of Mr. Roberts. So, ah, finally they asked me to come down to the police station. . . . [W]e talked for several hours, we went out to lunch, we talked some more, we came back and I said, 'You don't believe me, do you?' And they said, 'Well, really there's some questions here we feel you should know the answers to that you say you don't.' And I said, 'Fine do you have a polygraph here?'"

Walter Muellenhagen passed his polygraph test, and from then on the polygraph was a tool detectives used freely. That same week Monnie Bliss also agreed to be polygraphed. Just like Muellenhagen, he passed.

Next the detectives took a closer look at Dick.

* * *

On the last afternoon of his life, Dick was dressed for travel. He was wearing a beige safari jacket over a white short-sleeved knit shirt. In the pocket of his black trousers police found a plastic comb, a white handkerchief, a jackknife, and eighty-three cents. On his feet were a pair of ankle-high doeskin dress boots, brand name After Hours. As for jewelry, he wore his gold wedding band on his left hand and a Masonic ring set with a gem-cut blue stone on his right.

Dick was wearing exactly what a man of leisure, ready for a trip, should be. Nothing telling, nothing out of the ordinary. Except for one little item that didn't attract attention until long after the autopsy, when the Robisons' extended family asked that Dick's personal effects be released and returned to them. Suspended on a thin chain around Dick's neck, invisible until the medical examiner removed the dead man's shirt and jacket, had been a round gold disk. The disk was a St. Christopher medal with this perplexing inscription in an uneven scrawl scratched on the back: "Richard to my chosen son and heir—God bless you. Roebert."

The name Christopher means "Christ carrier" in Greek, and Catholics revere St. Christopher as the patron saint of travelers. He is also sometimes invoked, the *New Catholic Dictionary* says, to ward off "sudden death."

Still, detectives didn't know what to make of Dick's religious necklace. St. Christopher medals were popular in the 1960s; mothers would give them to their children as a protective talisman, and boys would give them to their sweethearts to show that they were going steady. Dick was a devout Lutheran, though, not a Catholic, and this was no gift from a silly crush. As far as his lineage was concerned, detectives knew he was the son of Ross Robison, and not of a man named Roebert. Police wondered who this mystery man was, what his relationship with Dick was, and why he would give Robison something as intimate as a piece of jewelry—religious jewelry at that.

It surprised some family members, too.

"We were shocked . . . when we heard about it," Shirley's mother, Aileen Fulton, told a reporter. "That Richard would be carrying that medal

with that writing or inscription or whatever behind it. We never knew anything about that. We still can't figure it out."

In their search of Dick's office at R. C. Robison and Associates,
Stearns and Flis found a clue. It was a weirdly rambling, six-page letter addressed to "Roebert (My Father)," dated May 17, 1968, handwritten on *Impresario* magazine stationery and signed by Dick.

"I'm most honored and pleased with the message given me by 'Steam-
boat Joe' this morning," the letter begins.

> I have it where we decided and have instructed Joe not to allow me
> to "drop my wallet." Also, if something (how?) should happen to
> me to take the entire wallet and pass it "up" to where the Moter
> [*sic*] people would know what to do with it.

The letter goes on to mention the car allowances Dick has given two
members of his staff, *Impresario* executive editor Ted Seemeyer and managing editor Ernest Gilbert, as part of their newly increased salary pack-
ages, and names their choices in automobiles. The letter continues:

> Now . . . a favorite story of mine was the one where a fellow ar-
> rived at work excited about the "Tremendous" collision that must
> have taken place on the company's corner earlier. No one was
> aware of it . . . but he insisted a Mustang and a Thunderbird had to
> have hit head on 'cause there were feathers and horse [manure] all
> over the place. Now . . . it should prove, in the future, most inter-
> esting to see whether we have a similar mess strewn about the halls
> of "Ole Impresario" via Ted the Mustang and Ernie the Thunder-
> bird. It will be interesting to see if wonderful "Steamboat" has a
> keen sense of smell.

Dick closes the letter, "I thank God for you, father. Your son always,
Richard." Then in a postscript he writes, "Incidentally, 'Ole Joe' really had
a 'full head o steam' this time. He was MOST controlled!" Then he finally
concludes, "I'm looking forward with great anticipation and love to the day
when we finally meet—soon I hope. Always—your son Richard."

A state police handwriting expert and document examiner confirmed
that the letter was not a forgery but had indeed been written by Dick.
With that, detectives began to have doubts about the man's sanity—
doubts inspired by this bizarre letter, but also by the divergent opinions
about Dick's character expressed by those closest to him, as well as the first

hints of a multi-million-dollar business enterprise Dick was supposedly hatching with no documentation to back it up. Detectives were further perplexed by the words of Dick's own Lutheran minister.

"Dick was a strict parent, a brilliant and determined individual, but he had a split personality," Pastor Harvey Peters of the Calvary Lutheran Church in Southfield told the detectives. Peters had known Dick since the Robison family joined his congregation. Peters admired Dick's intelligence and his faith, but said that he had an abrasive personality and was "kind of a Dr. Jekyll and Mr. Hyde type."

Reverend Peters had presided at the Robison family's funeral and was forthcoming with his opinions. Though Peters was an admirer of Dick, he said he was an abrasive person who "couldn't even win an election to the church council of the congregation he helped form in 1958."

Dick didn't work well as part of a team, and so Reverend Peters gave him solo projects, saying he was inwardly warm but guarded his emotions in front of others. Though the family never missed attending services when they were in town, Dick would often avoid the traditional after-service handshake.

"He would sometimes scoot out the side door and not shake hands," Reverend Peters said. "But then he might call me later in the week to say hello or to take me to lunch."

With the assistance of Emmet County sheriff's deputies, local police officers, and state troopers normally assigned to patrol highways, detectives planned to check out a number of men with varied psychiatric histories, some violent and some just pitiable, in the event that a homicidal madman was roaming the north country, seeking out his next victim randomly. First though, there was one man whose mental health detectives needed to check the status of. That man was Dick Robison himself.

On October 7, 1968, Detectives Stearns and Flis contacted the head man at the Ypsilanti State Hospital, Dr. Alexander Dukay, and requested his help. From 1931 until it was demolished to make way for a Toyota automotive plant in 2005, the Ypsilanti State Hospital was not only a cavernous brick campus that housed four thousand mentally ill patients, but was also home to one of the state's Centers for Forensic Psychiatry. A small area out back, called the "back ward" by staff and the "snake pit" by patients, was circled with barbed wire and contained some of the state's most twisted criminals, deemed, because of the depravity of their crimes, to be criminally insane.

These patients and the motives for their crimes were studied by staff psychiatrists, and any valuable information gleaned was regularly passed on to law enforcement personnel. Detectives Stearns and Flis approached Dr. Dukay with a folder of material on Dick Robison, in the event that the doctor might be able to categorize their increasingly mysterious victim. They gave the doctor copies of the editorials Dick wrote for *Impresario*, other miscellaneous writings they found in his home and office, and brought him up to date on the investigation.

The text of one of Dick's editorials in the April 1967 issue of the magazine did sound a bit angry. The "hoax-art" being criticized was works of greatness by such painters as Pablo Picasso, Jasper Johns, and Paul Klee.

Although it's difficult, at times, to turn our cheek when being hit in the face by some of the obvious hoax-art that has been given credence of late by those who either know and don't care or those who don't know and care less, we take comfort in the fact that in the light of cold objectivity, art of nothingness remains . . . nothingness.

Another, in February 1968 stated, "A fact of great significance that should interest you as a reader of *Impresario* is the finding that more acclaim has been attached to *Impresario* Readers as the thought-provoking leaders of our fair country. You earn more, spend more, know more and read *Impresario* better than any other magazine reader in the land."

Dick would end each of these missives with his signature tagline: "Until next time remember . . . think a little . . . it's a free man's responsibility. RCR."

After reviewing all of the material given to him by detectives, Dr. Dukay told the men that in his professional opinion, Dick Robison was a "brilliant intellectual" but also "mentally disturbed."

"Mentally disturbed" was not a diagnosis that doctors who worked at the Ypsilanti State Hospital were strangers to. Before psychiatric drugs became widely available, those who treated the mentally ill resorted to extreme measures in an attempt to find something that would help their patients. Ypsilanti patients were subjected to warm baths and then wrapped in cold wet sheets as part of something called "hydrotherapy." Some were exposed to various spectrums of light, or physiotherapy, and even purposely infected with malaria. Patients who didn't respond to this treatment were candidates for lobotomies and electroshock therapy. With such extreme treatment at his legal disposal, Dr. Dukay certainly had an opportunity to view all types of mental disturbances, and it was doubtful he gave the diagnosis of Dick Robison lightly.

According to their August 6, 1968, report, someone else told Stearns and Flis that Dick had mental problems, though the detectives didn't reveal their source. "During this investigation information was received that Mr. Robison may have been treated by a member of the psychiatric staff of the Oakwood Hospital in Dearborn," officers wrote. "This information found that he was mentally ill and recommendations were made to the family to have him committed. . . . [A]s of this date, no information has been found to substantiate this rumor."

Dr. Dukay is one likely source of this rumor. The report of the detectives' interview with Dr. Dukay and the report of the rumor were documented consecutively in the official police report filed by Stearns and Flis and logged on the same day. However, the detectives were unable to substantiate the rumor. Oakwood Hospital, the Dearborn facility that supposedly employed the psychiatrist who recommended the commitment, had no record of treating a Dick Robison as either an inpatient or an outpatient.

While looking to the mental health community for a clear picture of the man, detectives instead came face to face with the duplicitous nature of Dick Robison. He was either prudently careful or paranoid, rude or a man of high principles, a visionary or a nutcase. Detectives had been untangling this dead man's life and following each thread to its frayed conclusion yet they still hadn't figured Dick out. The motive for his murder, and that of his wife and children, remained somewhere in the knot of this brilliant but disturbed husband, father, and businessman they still couldn't get a handle on.

The Mentals

1968

Believing the murders were committed
by a person with a deranged mind,
law enforcement agencies in
Northern Michigan swept up every
possible suspect.

—*Detroit News,* January 6, 1970

Sixty miles southwest of Good Hart on the outskirts of downtown Traverse City looms the Northern Michigan Asylum for the Insane. Built in 1885 under the guidance of eminent psychiatrist Thomas Story Kirkbride, the original buildings have the long halls, tall windows, and spacious interiors he advocated, his theory being that psychiatric hospital structures could have a curative effect on the patients committed there. Their very bricks and mortar were "a special apparatus for the care of lunacy."

The facility was renamed the Traverse City State Hospital in the early 1900s, when the rambling Victorian buildings housed a sorrowful assortment of not only the mentally ill but also those afflicted with tuberculosis, epilepsy, typhoid, diphtheria, influenza, and polio. Even some infirm and elderly nurses with no other prospects found end-of-life shelter here. By the late 1970s the enormous Kirkbride buildings were abandoned in favor of smaller, less expensive, and easier to maintain cottages. The state hospital closed in 1989, by which time many of the remaining patients were being treated with newly developed pharmaceuticals. Drugs were in; asylums had gone out of fashion. Today the facility has found new life as a retail, residential, and professional development.

From the summer of 1968 until the early 1970s, a galaxy of newly released mental hospital patients, hitchhikers, hobos, alcoholics, escapees, fugitives, and wanderers, many with ties to Traverse City's State Hospital, were investigated by both the Emmet County Sheriff's Office and the Michigan State Police. If the target of the crime wasn't Dick, perhaps the killer was criminally insane. In those unenlightened times, despite the severity of their diagnosis or the intensity of their suffering, each was officially labeled by law enforcement as simply "a mental."

The first of these was Jay Freeman, who left the state hospital in late June 1968, then inexplicably applied for a six-hundred-dollar loan from the Associates Finance Corporation in Traverse City. The loan officer, Jerry Lounsberry, ran the required credit check and found that Freeman rather poorly fit the company's profile of a good loan risk. Not only had he spent time in Southern Michigan Prison, but his most recent address was "Inmate, Traverse City State Hospital."

"He was hard to get along with and very demanding about getting the money," Lounsberry told the Michigan State Police. While in the state hospital, Freeman had been overheard saying that he had "threatened some wealthy people in the Petoskey area for money." Freeman was eliminated as a suspect when hospital records showed that he had been released into the care of his guardian on June 28, 1968, four days after the murders.

The next possibility came through an anonymous tip to police on August 12, 1968, naming Richard Fowler Wines of Good Hart. Wines was a junior at Olivet College, in downstate Michigan, who was working at the Boyne Highlands resort in Harbor Springs as a busboy for the summer. He had spent time in a mental institution, and for that reason alone was a valid suspect. Captain Raymond H. McConnell of the state police interviewed Wines, who readily admitted that he was a "schizophrenic homicidal" and volunteered that he had spent two months in Mercywood Sanitarium in Ann Arbor. McConnell and another officer searched the cabin where Wines lived, owned by his eighty-four-year-old grandmother, and found neither guns nor anything else suspicious. Clifford Fosmore meanwhile interviewed Wine's friend, Bruce Corpe of Harbor Springs, who said that in recent days Wines had been consumed with his plans to get married and had been working long hours in order to make enough money to pay for the wedding.

"He is the type of person that, had he done it, he would have been all upset for days," said Corpe, who worked alongside Wines at the skiing and golfing resort and had not observed any troubling behavior. A check of his time sheet showed that Wines had clocked nearly thirty hours on the job from June 24 through June 26, and he was cleared.

Closer to the actual crime, in both timing and geography, was the thirty-nine-year-old self-employed tree trimmer, Russell Dale Figg. Figg had been hired by Dick Robison to trim trees around the Robison cottage and was one of the last people to see the family alive. Police interviewed Figg the day after the murders were discovered, but talked to him again after the emotionally charged phone call he made to the state police post in Petoskey.

"There's something bothering my conscience," he told the person who answered the call. That was enough to spur Troopers John F. Furecic and Edward Hancock to make a trip to Figg's home on U.S. 31. Figg told the two troopers that he had worked from 9:30 a.m. to 4:00 p.m. on both Tuesday, June 25, the presumed day of the murders, and Wednesday, June 26. As he was going about his work he saw the Robisons on June 25, he said, but not on June 26.

"The reason I called you, what's bothering my conscience, is that in my own mind I wonder if maybe the mother was being held as a hostage while I was outside working and I didn't even know it," Figg said.

Figg related that the Robison family was home on Tuesday, June 25, but that he did not see Shirley Robison or her young daughter. He said he saw Dick and all three of the Robison boys on numerous occasions during that day, and that his teenaged helper, Allan Elya Jr., had seen a little girl watching them work from an upstairs window, but neither one saw Shirley Robison. Figg said that by Wednesday morning, June 26, when he and Elya started work, the place was quiet and even though there were two cars parked in the driveway, somehow it still looked like no one was home.

On July 25, 1968, troopers reinterviewed Figg, this time at the police post. They had found out that he was recently divorced, and that his marriage had not ended civilly. Figg submitted a handwriting sample, was fingerprinted, and his shoes were examined to see if they had left the bloody footprints. Figg agreed to take a polygraph test and one was scheduled for July 27. The day before the polygraph, Trooper Gunnard Dahl from the Grand Haven post interviewed Figg's ex-wife, Donna Gardner, in her Ravenna home. According to the daily report filed by Dahl, the discussion went like this:

Dahl: Why did you divorce your husband?
Gardner: Because of his violent temper. It got worse when I was
    pregnant. Once, just after our son John was born, I washed
    some diapers but forgot to hang them up to dry. He went
    into a fit of rage. He could get so violent over the slightest
    little things.
Dahl: Did Mr. Figg ever receive any psychiatric treatment that
    you know of?
Gardner: Oh yeah, for three or four months in either 1958 or
    1959, I can't remember which. And before that he was in the
    Army, and I think he had to get treatment then, too.
Dahl: Do you consider him to be a dangerous person?

Gardner: Just to himself. Back in 1961 he went over to Camps
    Drug Store, pulled a bottle of acid off the shelf, and drank it.
Dahl: Why would he do something like that?
Gardner: Because I told him that I wanted a divorce.

On July 27, Figg showed up at the post at the allotted time for his lie detector test, and polygraph administrator Robert Ferry duly connected him to the apparatus. Ferry inquired after Figg's activities on June 25 and 26. "Did you kill the Robisons?" the examiner asked. Figg denied knowing anything about the murders. He was found to be truthful in all of his answers, and after his teenaged helper corroborated his account of their activities, Figg was cleared of any involvement.

In the village of Good Hart, however, with no clear suspect identified, suspicions were beginning to build unchecked. In the week following the discovery of the crime neighbors reported on neighbors, drinking buddies looked cross-eyed at one another, and a facial tic or twitchy eyes were enough to arouse the attention of police. Even in such a climate of widespread suspicion, Esther Williams of Petoskey was unusually vigilant: she the only mother to turn in her own sons. Two out of four of them, anyway. Marvin and Skippy, she said, were just no good.

Marvin E. Williams, twenty-eight, was a past inmate of the Traverse City State Hospital and was on parole for aggravated assault and breaking and entering; his brother Harold "Skippy" Williams, twenty-six, was also on parole. Both were under the supervision of parole officer John Sweet. As part of his rehabilitation, Marvin was enrolled in a sewing class at Petoskey Junior College, and Skippy was supposed to be seeking employment as a cook or baker, two vocations he learned in the prison kitchen. Instead, both headed for Detroit, where local police fielded rumors that Skippy had "purchased a gun, and was going to do a lot of damage with it."

On July 30 Esther Williams called police and said that she thought either one of her sons, or even the two working together, could have committed the murders. "Both of the boys would do this kind of thing," she said. "They're vicious. A few years back, Harold rode by a house and shot out the windows. And there was a babysitter in the house at the time." Marvin, too, had a history of violence. In addition to his time in prison and Traverse City State Hospital, he had been sent to Lapeer Mental Hospital after attacking his mother with a knife.

The police obtained arrest warrants for violation of parole, charging the errant brothers with absconding from supervision. Marvin was arrested in Room 58 at the Vernon Hotel in Highland Park, near Detroit, on

August 1 and his little brother, Skippy, was arrested two days later in Hazel Park, a few miles away. Both were polygraphed and cleared of suspicion of murdering the Robisons.

On another anonymous tip, police camped out in the records room of the Traverse City State Hospital and combed through the treatment records of Charles W. Thornton, a twenty-nine-year-old man in and out of the hospital over the four years preceding the crime. Thornton had first been committed to the state hospital on October 19, 1964, on a six-day emergency petition from the Petoskey courts. The petition stated that Thornton had assaulted his wife, his mother, and his stepfather numerous times, once breaking his mother's arm. Thornton's doctor reported that the patient "believes he has two minds, but that he has both under control." Thornton, however, proved to be a dead end. He had an alibi and no known connection to the victims.

While examining Thornton's records, officers also came upon others: an escapee from the hospital in July, arrested in August in Manistee for drunk and disorderly; a man from Good Hart, labeled "a mental" and confined to the hospital at the time of the murders; a patient from Harbor Springs, AWOL from the army; a twenty-nine-year-old former patient with "red kinky hair, one eye with a constant twitch"; a window-peeper; a "passive aggressive type" who had been committed after holding his parents in their Boyne Falls trailer at gunpoint; a man treated at Wayne County General Hospital and arrested in Charlevoix for reckless driving, who reportedly had "a very foul mouth and talks freely about his sex problems that are other than normal." When officers contacted the manager of the apartment where he lived, they were told that he was "harassing and making advances at the lady tenants and appears to be having another breakdown."

Each one of this group of ne'er-do-wells was questioned and was found to have an alibi and to have no ties to any of the Robisons. To a man they were cleared.

The Phony

1968

You're not filling us in on a lot
of this stuff. I can tell you right
now, I don't know why you're doing
it, I don't know what your reason is,
but I'll tell you right now, it's
not good.

> —Detective Lloyd Stearns interviewing Joe Scolaro,
> August 7, 1968

Dick Robison had a "right-hand man," and his name was Joseph Raymond Scolaro III; by his own admission he was a liar, a cheat, and a phony. At six feet and two hundred pounds, with greased black hair, tailored jackets, and blackish eyes that watched everything behind dark-framed glasses, Joseph "Joe" Scolaro was flashy and slick. Dick hired the thirty-year-old, go-getting army veteran in December 1965 as one of the first employees at R. C. Robison and Associates.

"I like the cut of your cloth," Robison told Scolaro, a suit-and-tie man from the day he shed his army uniform. "I want you to go to work for me."

Despite the Robison firm's urbane-sounding name, up until that point the business had mostly been a one-man operation with Robison alone securing new clients, selling ads, and acting as both editor and publisher of *Impresario*. The hiring of Joe would make the word "Associates" in his firm's name not an empty term used to make the enterprise sound more important, but a reality.

Though hired on a handshake months ago, Joe's official start date was sometime in March 1965; his pay was based on commission, but he took a draw of $850 a month to start.

For ten years Robison had been building both his reputation and client list, beginning in 1955 when, as a fresh-faced and energetic ad man he gained the trust of the men behind his first major account, Delta Faucet. Engineers there had reworked the traditional sink faucet using a patented single-handle design, and the marketing people wanted to get the word out about their new product. Dick was happy to oblige, and over the next twelve years came to think of the advertising placement work he did for the plumbing fixture company as his bread and butter.

Landing Delta was a coup for the young Dick Robison; Delta was a division of Masco Corporation, the industrial powerhouse founded by the Armenian immigrant and entrepreneur Alex Manoogian, a philanthropist who later donated his riverfront mansion to the city of Detroit to be used as the mayor's residence.

A landscape painter and a fan of the opera, Dick had big plans for his fledgling enterprise, and dreamed of expanding the firm from representing a few regional advertising clients and publishing a local arts magazine into a cultural empire, complete with urban arts centers, student scholarships, and international performing arts tours. If he was going to build such an empire, Robison needed a lot more clients like Alex Manoogian's Delta Faucet, and so he hired Joe to help land them.

"The chemistry was right and we liked each other from the very beginning," Joe would later tell police. "There was a small pay cut for the first check and then every check after that he kept increasing it. He gave me a check for two thousand dollars and I said 'How long is this going to last?' and he said, 'You know me, everything lasts forever.'"

To Dick, Joe must have looked good on paper. A year of college at Harvard University, where he studied business and marketing. Sales experience and contacts from his work as an advertising broker, selling ad space to up-and-coming businesses in the Detroit area and then placing those ads within a variety of suitable publications, including the *Birmingham Eccentric*. Joe had learned the business from his father, J. Raymond Scolaro, Jr., who was manager of Grit Publishing Company and a member of the Adcraft Club in Detroit.

When he was serving his country in the army, Joe was clever enough to have been selected for a secret spy branch of the military, and though he may have come across as a bit sly, he was also a family man with a new wife, a young son, and plans for more children. This in particular would have endeared him to Dick, who was proud of his own brood of well-mannered children and of his stylish wife. The two couples became friendly, getting together for dinners at home and weekend morning coffees.

"He was a genius," Joe would tell anyone who would listen—reporters, cops, colleagues—in the days after the murders. "He's one of the greatest guys I ever met in my life. He adopted me like a son, though our ages weren't that far apart. Later, we were like brothers. We were inseparable for three and a half years. We did things personally together, we ate lunch together, we spent every moment together."

Within a month of hiring Joe, however, R. C. Robison and Associates' finances started looking hinky. Police determined that from early in 1966 to June 1968, when the company came to a standstill after the murders, clients were being overbilled, bootleg advertisements from prominent airlines like Pan Am and United were being run pro bono in *Impresario,* without the companies' approval or knowledge, and printing bills were being paid late or not paid at all.

A United Airlines public relations man told detectives that Joe had solicited all of the airlines to purchase advertising space in the magazine. "All refused but he went ahead and ran the ad and then sent them bills for it," the man said. "In United's case, they called Robison to ask why and to refuse to pay. Robison replied, 'Oh, there has been some mistake; just ignore the bill.'"

By the end of 1968, police found that by the first quarter of that year, Dick's signature client, Delta Faucet, had been swindled out of more than $50,000 in ad money. During the same time period, $60,000 in advertising bills from publications in which R. C. Robison and Associates had placed ads for clients, and even received the money to purchase the space, were unpaid. From January through June 1968, just $3,500 in legitimate advertising was sold.

Chrysler advertised in *Impresario,* and so did the trust department of the National Bank of Detroit. Lincoln advertised its Continental, and Chudiks of Birmingham informed women shoppers that "summer elegance" was in. Meadowbrook Theater announced its new season, and Planned Auto Management offered readers leases on a Buick Wildcat two-door hardtop for $93.75 a month, or a Ford Mustang two-door hardtop for $83 a month. These ads appeared to be legitimate, though detectives couldn't be certain. After all, Dick was a client of the National Bank of Detroit, and both he and Joe leased their cars from Planned Auto Management.

"We never suspected anything until the police came to see us the spring after the murders," Richard Manoogian, Alex Manoogian's son, told reporters. "We just took Dick's word for it when he sent in the budget."

Eight months before the murder, Dick hired a Bloomfield Hills, Michigan, financial planner and insurance expert, Phillip Skillman, to conduct an estate plan. Skillman, a representative of New York Life Insurance, was also a regular advertiser in *Impresario,* cautioning readers, "Your estate plan may need a review."

According to the documents Dick furnished for Skillman to conduct his work, Dick himself valued his two businesses, the magazine and the ad firm, at $600,000.

The financial downturn began months earlier, but Dick probably first learned of it early in the morning on June 25, 1968. The day police believed he and his family were murdered, Dick called his banker, Frank Joity at the National Bank of Detroit, to check on an expected $200,000 deposit and was told it had not been made and that the balance in his company's checking account was just $15,000.

Between his conversation with his banker and the murder, a period of not more than ten hours, Dick exchanged seventeen phone calls with Joe Scolaro. The subject of the phone calls can only be surmised, but the missing money surely came up.

Still, Joe expressed disbelief when questioned by police about the missing money. Financial matters were handled by Dick and the accountant, Cal Mackey, he said. Mackey initially refused to talk, and so whether or not Dick knew about or masterminded the overcharges, the accounting irregularities, the unpaid bills, or any of the other financial flimflam, it was impossible for detectives to determine.

They did know, however, that in the decade before Joe was hired, no complaints were ever recorded about Dick's business practices—not from Delta Faucet or from anyone else. For his part, Joe stressed to police that he purposely stayed out of the finances, and made especially certain to keep his distance from Harry Ford, their Delta Faucet contact.

"As far as the big one, Harry Ford, I stayed away from him," Joe told police. "Dick wanted to be the only one who had the connection with him. He wanted things done a certain way to fit his pattern. Dick always had the attitude that no matter what, he could never lose the Delta account. I wasn't involved with any of the billing, either. Dick handled that. Dick and Cal."

This didn't quite square with what police suspected about the way Dick had been conducting his business or with what Joe had told them himself in earlier interviews. In April 1968, when the kids were on Easter break, Dick took his whole family on a two-week trip to Hawaii, and right before they left, Joe said, Dick turned the day-to-day operation of the magazine and the advertising firm over to him. Dick even told Joe that he had become as indispensable as "his right arm."

The new responsibilities for Joe lasted not just for the duration of the Hawaii trip, but for good. Cal Mackey would continue to handle the finances, but Joe was in charge of everything else. Joe might not have spoken with Harry Ford directly, but he knew all about the account. Dick had begun to work on a business idea that he said might finance his dream of supporting the arts with urban cultural centers, and he needed to free up his time and his mental energy to put this idea in motion.

And he made good on his promise to cut back his time in the office. Between returning from Hawaii in mid-April and leaving for Good Hart in mid-June, Dick was spending only two days a week in his office, and some weeks not even that much. Joe was in the office Monday through Friday, and sometimes came in on Saturdays. He had keys to the outer doors and possession of the company checkbook—though not permission to write checks. He supervised the other employees, checked the mail, and he drafted much of Dick's correspondence. In return for these increased responsibilities, Joe said, he was given a $700-a-week raise and was promised a 20 percent share of both businesses.

The inconsistencies in Joe's story, and the timing of the missing money, were not lost on police, and Dick's right-hand man soon became one of the Michigan State Police's most watched men.

"We figure you're a suspect in this thing now," Detective Stearns told Joe during one of his many interrogations. "And very strongly so because of all the discrepancies we've found."

Stearns talked to Joe's wife, Lora Lee, and to his neighbors. He questioned his mother, Kathleen "Kitty" Scolaro, and his business associates. He reinterviewed the people Scolaro worked with at the Robison firm. He and Detective Flis followed Joe around town sometimes in a police cruiser, sometimes in an unmarked car, making no attempt to disguise their presence. They paid surprise visits to his office during business hours. They called him at home, in the evening and on weekends. When they felt like it, they even walked up to him on the street and struck up a conversation, sometimes just talking about the weather and not even bringing up the murders.

While the police followed Joe, reporters followed the police: "When he goes on a trip, the police know where he is. When he buys a new car, the police write down its license number. And when he talks about Dick Robison . . . the police listen carefully to every word," reported the *Detroit Free Press.*

* * *

Joe's life hadn't always been lived like that of a hunted animal. A son of Michigan, born in Detroit on May 10, 1938, as a tall and bookish-looking eighteen-year-old he enlisted in the U.S. Army immediately after graduating from high school. He was plucked from the ranks of generic recruits when officers saw his score on the military's standard intelligence test. In basic training, Joe learned to carry, clean, and shoot a gun, but was assigned to the Army Security Agency (ASA) and given a J-38—a Morse code "straight key"—and taught how to use it. The ASA was the new and secretive branch of military intelligence that has since morphed into today's powerful National Security Agency.

In the fall of 1956, Joe was trained as a Morse code intercept operator and sent to Japan, along with fellow soldiers in his unit who had been trained in a variety of intelligence-gathering methods including linguistics and cryptology. Their charge was to seize Cold War communist communications from the airwaves, decode them, and report their findings. Joe's service to his country began on September 10, 1956, his tour of duty sandwiched between the Korean War and the Vietnam War. A little earlier or later, and this work would likely have been substantially more perilous. During the Korean War, he could have been planting movement detection devices underground along the Korean border. A little later, and he could have been locating Viet Cong radio transmitters—the assignment that resulted in the first recorded American casualty of the Vietnam War, an ASA soldier killed on the outskirts of Saigon on December 22, 1961.

Because their work was so hidden, even from other military personnel, ASA field soldiers like Joe Scolaro were known within the armed forces as the "Clandestine Warriors." The shoulder insignia they wore on their uniforms depicted the black-feathered leg of an eagle, talons tightly grasping two lightning bolts, the eagle leg symbolizing the strength of the army and the lightning bolts their electronic warfare capabilities. Scolaro's last assignment was to the Twelfth ASA Field Station in Japan, and he was given top secret clearance. He received an honorable discharge on July 14, 1959 with a rank of SP-4.

It takes a special kind of mind to decipher Morse code. First, you have to translate short and long sounds or electronic pulses, as well as the gaps between them, into letters of the alphabet and elements of punctuation. Then, you have to translate those letters into words, and finally be able to put those words into meaningful sentences. Memorization forms the base of the ability, but it is a physical skill as well.

Though developed in the 1940s for use with Samuel Morse's telegraph machine, Morse code is considered an early form of digital communication because it uses just two states—off and on—to communicate. It is the only form of digital communication in which the parties do not need a computer. Those who are accomplished at reading Morse code are themselves the computer, and Joe must have possessed a special kind of mind, because it was a skill that he mastered and one that certainly intrigued the state police detectives—intrigued them enough for a steamed-up Detective Stearns to make the following short speech to Joe during one of his many formal interrogations:

Here's the thing now. You have been in an organization that deals basically with the same type of work that we do, military intelligence. You know damn well that we work on real close information. On minute detail. Yet, you're not filling us in on minute details and these are the things that we've got to know, we want to know. I don't know why you're doing it, I don't know what your reason is, but I'll tell you right now, it's not good. So for whatever reason you're holding this kind of stuff back from us, I don't know, but at this time, we are going to advise you of your rights. We feel that we are getting a lot of horseshit from you. We don't want any more of it. We are done playing cat and mouse. Do you remember your rights at all? Do you remember these? You have the right to remain silent. Anything you say can and will be used against you in a court of law. You have the right to talk to a lawyer and have him present with you while you are being questioned. If you cannot afford to hire a lawyer, one will be appointed to represent you before any questioning if you wish one. You can decide anytime to exercise these rights and not answer any questions or make any statements. Now, do you understand these? Okay, having understood these, do you wish to exercise any of them now?

"No," said Joe calmly. "I've got nothing to hide."

1968

There are many unanswered questions in
the case, the biggest mystery ever in
the north woods around this two-pump
town in the heart of Northern
Michigan's gun country.

—UPI reporter Andrew R. McGill, July 28, 1968

Good Hart was indeed a two-pump town in 1968. And while most communities on northern Michigan's tourist coast have grown bigger and more modern in the past forty years, today Good Hart is a no-pump town. The two gas pumps that stood like vintage sentries in front of the General Store for nearly a half century were turned off more than a decade ago for a bureaucratic tangle of environmental, legal, political, and financial reasons.

The first owner of the General Store, Cliff Powers, installed the pumps in the 1950s when RV-ing was starting to become popular. Back then, the arrival of summer weather was just beginning to bring with it a constant silvery stream of station wagons pulling Airstream travel trailers behind them up the hill into town like a school of alewives. These rigs burned sometimes double the gas of an automobile alone and needed frequent fill-ups. Cliff Powers saw the future drive by the front of his little store, wanted it to stop off long enough to shop a little, and so in went the gas pumps.

The store's current owners, Carolyn and Jim Sutherland, turned off the pumps in 1997 and had them and their attending thousand-gallon gasoline storage tank removed in order to satisfy the State of Michigan's changing environmental regulations. Today, if you're in downtown Good Hart and need gas, you can head either north eight miles to the gas station and minimart in Cross Village, or south twenty miles to Harbor Springs.

The guns, though, never left town. This is still the heart of the Lower Peninsula's gun country.

The most obvious reason for the number of guns registered in the northern part of the state is hunting. Northern Michigan has a long and equally proud tradition of supporting hunters and hunting. There are legal seasons here for black bear, elk, deer, turkey, muskrat, mink, bobcat, raccoon, badger, beaver, otter, woodchuck, rabbit, squirrel, and even skunk. There are still a few residents around Good Hart and Cross Village who feed themselves and their families just fine and yet have never bought meat from a store.

As for the northern Michigan skies, hunters' guns are sighted on American woodcocks, ring-necked pheasants, quail, grouse, starlings, sparrows, feral pigeons, and crows. You can't hunt songbirds in the state, or eagles, hawks, owls, or swans. Voters turned down a petition recently to hunt doves—not sporting and not enough meat. Some four-footed creatures are protected too, including wolverines, wolves, lynx, moose, cougars, fox, and mother bears and cubs.

More than seven hundred thousand people a year hunt white tail deer in Michigan, the state with more public land available for hunting than any other east of the Mississippi River, according to the Department of Natural Resources. For those who like to shoot, there are plenty of furred and feathered targets, and with Emmet County's dense woods, open fields, rambling ancient orchards, and inland lakes, populations of many game species are particularly healthy. While some things have changed in the forty years since the murder, a lot of them have not, and gun ownership is one.

The close accuracy of the local anecdotal statistic—that investigating officers would find "a gun in every house"—did not make their search for the murder weapon any easier. From the shell casings found at the scene, Detectives Stearns and Flis knew they were looking for a rifle and a handgun. The makes and models of these guns were unknown to officers, however, and with the sage words of the crime lab's Hugh Fish ringing in their ears, they looked for not just a suspect or suspects, but the murder weapons as well: "No suspected weapon in this case should be overlooked," Trooper Fish had advised anyone working the case. An admirable guidepost and one the detectives committed themselves to following, despite entering Good Hart's forest of weapons, mostly populated with rifles and shotguns.

Besides the blood-spattered claw hammer found at the scene, the first mention of any specific weapon in the investigation came from the lips of Joe Scolaro. During their first interview with him on July 23, 1968, at the Emmet County Sheriff's Office, Joe told police about two handguns he bought in the spring of 1968. They were two nine-shot semiautomatic .25-caliber Berettas that Joe had bought from a gun dealer friend, one for himself and one for Dick. He said he had also purchased one hundred rounds of Sako brand ammunition. Still wary after the violent Detroit riots, Dick told Joe he wanted a gun for personal protection. As long as he was buying one for Dick, Joe told the detectives, he decided to get one for himself, too.

The next day, back in Detroit, police collected Joe's Beretta and turned it over to Trooper Fish for analysis at the state police crime lab. Dick's matching gun, however, was nowhere to be found. It was not in the cottage, not in either of the Robison cars parked in the driveway, not at his Lathrup Village home, nor anywhere in his office. If Dick had indeed bought the gun for personal protection, it had failed miserably to protect him. Detectives must have thought it odd that it wasn't found at the crime scene. The handgun should have been in a drawer at Summerset or inside one of the car's glove boxes; somewhere easily accessible in the event of imminent danger. Unless, of course, it was one of the murder weapons.

All but one of the .25-caliber bullets collected at the cottage and tested by Fish were found to be badly mutilated, unusable for any forensic work. One bullet, however, was in good enough shape to provide Fish with a clear picture of its singular characteristics. This bullet had been fired from a gun exhibiting a signature of "six lands and grooves possibly with a left twist," he determined.

One good bullet was enough for Fish to suggest that the .25-caliber bullets from the floor, walls, upholstery, and grounds of the cottage and the .25-caliber bullets recovered from the bodies of the Robisons during their autopsies had all been fired from the same handgun. And there was something else. The bullets were, Fish noted, "characteristic of foreign ammunition." The hundred rounds of ammunition Scolaro bought along with the two Berettas were made by Sako, an uncommon brand manufactured in Finland.

Scolaro's confiscated Beretta was test-fired, and although it produced bullets strikingly similar to those found at the crime scene, they did not exactly match. With the evidence he had at hand, Fish could not say for certain that Dick Robison's missing gun was the murder weapon, but he could deduce that it was. The ".25 caliber fired bullets and shells exhibit class characteristics similar to the .25 automatic caliber Beretta pistol, #B47919, allegedly received from Mr. Scolaro," he wrote in his report. "However, the individual characteristics are dissimilar and this weapon is apparently not involved. This would indicate that the .25 automatic caliber Beretta pistol, #B47836, alleged to have been in the possession of Richard Robison, could be involved."

There was still a rifle to be considered, and until the police found it and Robison's handgun, any gun that seemed to intersect with the investigation, whether it was a handgun or rifle, was sent to either the Grayling or East Lansing crime labs and test-fired.

Even weapons that fired ammunition of a caliber thought to be unrelated were tested, in case they matched any other open investigation or in case new evidence came to light. In their attempt to find the murder weapons, detectives were not above randomly knocking on doors in the Good Hart area and asking whoever opened them if they could take a look at their guns. "But this gun is just a pea-shooter for varmints," countless Good Hart locals assured the officers, as they handed over their .22s.

Even these ancient and mostly unregistered rodent guns were handled by police as if one of them might be able to provide a crucial clue that would solve the case. And nothing, if it were connected to a firearm in any way, was above suspicion.

Just before the July 4 holiday weekend, a conservation officer patrolling forty miles east of Good Hart in Cheboygan State Park investigated an abandoned camping tent. Inside, he found a hunting jacket with 12-gauge shotgun shells in the pocket and identification for a Mark Wheeler. Further probing found that a Cheboygan police officer had made a traffic stop on a Mark Wheeler, noticed shotgun shells on the floor of his car, and asked to see inside the trunk. The 12-gauge Mossberg slide action shotgun they found when Wheeler opened it was confiscated and test-fired. No match to the Robison crime or any other open investigation.

At the Lasley house in Cross Village, officers talked to James, a college student at Eastern Michigan University, and he volunteered three .22s, which the officers test-fired, sending the spent shells to the crime lab in East Lansing. No match. Lasley's cousin, Samuel, volunteered his two .22s, but they were broken and not worth testing, detectives decided. Two of the boy's friends, Robert Kruzel of Cross Village and George Boynton of Harbor Springs, added the three .22s they owned between them. No match.

Monnie Bliss's .22 slide action Remington was checked and cleared, and so was Steve Shananaquet's .22 Winchester. Four full boxes of Western Super-X cartridges found in a closet at the Robison cottage were checked, and so were the fourteen loose cartridges of the same make found in a clothes hamper. No matches.

In August, Emmet County sheriff's deputies responded to a report of mailboxes being randomly shot up in a vandalism incident north of Good Hart. At the scene they collected ten .22-caliber Remington-Peters fired shells. No match.

A .25-caliber shell from a Colt semiautomatic pistol confiscated in a crime investigated by Southfield police was tested, and so was a .22-caliber fired bullet found inside a woman's purse that washed up along the shore of Lake Michigan. No match. Further tests were made on .22-caliber shells from a Stevens bolt action rifle, a Stevens Model 85, a Mossberg bolt action, a Remington Score Master, a Marlin single shot, and a Winchester Magnum. No matches.

Tree trimmer Russell Figg turned over his .22 Savage over and under. No match. Neighbors and family members weren't above suspicion, either. Robison's neighbor and friend Albert Little's .22 Winchester Model 06 pump action was checked, and so was the Ruger owned by Shirley Robison's brother, Marvin Fulton. No match on either one.

The owners of cottages in the immediate area were asked to turn in their weapons, too. A .22-caliber Spanish Star ten-shot pistol, a Ruger single six revolver, a J. C. Higgins nine-shot revolver, a .357 Colt Magnum, a Reck P-8 semiautomatic and a .38 Smith & Wesson were turned in, test-fired and compared with the crime scene evidence. No matches.

From there, the detectives' work to locate the murder weapons veered further afield. A disturbed man from Lakeview, three hundred miles from Good Hart, named James Robert Brant used a .25-caliber Beretta handgun to hold his parents in their trailer at gunpoint for reasons unknown. Brant was questioned and his gun was checked. No match.

William David Mann, owner of the gas station at Fingerboard Corners where M-68 meets M-33, volunteered his old Montgomery Ward .22, equipped with a scope, for no other reason than that two state troopers stopped by his place of business to make a phone call. No match.

Police from other jurisdictions got their two cents in, too. An officer with the Bureau of Criminal Identification and Investigation in London, Ohio, sent Trooper Fish suspicious shells fired from a .25-caliber Armi-Galesi automatic pistol. No match. A trooper from the Detroit post sent Fish shells test-fired from a Ruger Bearcat revolver. No match. A trooper from the Cadillac post sent in a .25 Beretta pistol picked up by request. A local man had called the post and told police that he owned a .25 Beretta he bought used; he had heard about the crime and wanted the gun checked. The gun was thought to be part of a stolen shipment when police looked up its serial number, but still no match.

By now, the ammunition from fifty-three guns of every make, model, caliber, and condition had been tested against the bullets and shell casings found at the crime scene. With the help of the keen eyes and exacting natures of those who ran the ballistics tests, Stearns and Flis had a good idea that the Robison family was killed with a .25-caliber Beretta handgun and a .22-caliber rifle. The detectives were certain that those guns had been in Good Hart on June 25, 1968. They just didn't know where they were now.

Following the Money

1968

> The solution to the Robison murders could well lie somewhere in the convoluted business dealings of Richard Robison. But it could also lie somewhere in the steep forests and shadowy headlands of the Good Hart area.
>
> —Bob Clock, *Petoskey News-Review,* July 21, 1978

A family of six was dead, and in the ensuing months that the crime remained unsolved, one of the most vexing things about the case for police was that they did not know exactly why the murders had been committed in the first place. The financial problems in Dick Robison's business affairs were just an educated guess.

In the past century experts in the fields of psychiatry and psychology have floated a variety of theories in an attempt to explain the motivations for human beings to kill. Some of these theories have proven meritorious over time, others only ridiculous.

In the Middle Ages and beyond, murder was blamed on demon possession, and once people believed that, there was little reason for them to inquire any further. Then in the early nineteenth century, phrenology came into fashion. Phrenology was the science of matching personality to human skull shapes—believers were convinced that the wrong bumps on one's noggin signaled a propensity to murder. Throughout the 1900s scientists and psychologists came up with various theories to explain murder, including "the bad seed"; the childhood psychopath; crime that ran in families (which helped explain the Mafia); a capitalistic society that rewarded ruthlessness; an extra Y chromosome; and adults in possession of a psyche marred forever by child abuse. Even poor nutrition was not overlooked—in the 1970s one defendant in California blamed his murderous crime on eating too many Twinkies.

Bunk, says Sheriff Pete Wallin, who is the current head lawman in Emmet County. As far as he is concerned, the primary role of law enforcement is to protect the innocent and serve the needs of the victims of violent crime and their families, instead of getting overly wrapped up with the psychological makeup of the perpetrators, unless of course it helps apprehend a criminal. Still, Wallin said, the four main motives for murder—greed, sex, jealousy, and money—can be distilled down to just money and sex.

"All kinds of people looking at this case over the years have come up with all these complicated motives, but most of the time, crime just isn't that way," Wallin says. "Dick Robison had some big business plans in the works, and I think the motive for his murder was just money, plain and simple."

From the chronology of the official reports, it would seem that his colleagues at the state police assigned to the case nearly forty years ago agreed with him. Dick Robison's money, and his supposed plans to make a lot more of it, grabbed police officers' attention from the very beginning.

"Dick Robison was a dreamer," Dick's accountant, Cal Mackey, told state police detectives. "He would dream on paper, you know, he could be a multi, multi billionaire, that was his ambition in life, to be like Howard Hughes."

Here was a man with a comfortable home in a Detroit suburb and a cottage on five lakeside lots in Good Hart. A man with two brand-new cars and his own airplane, a Cessna Sky Hawk. A man who supported his family in style, traveling with them on vacation to Hawaii, sending his oldest son to college and even talking of buying his young daughter not just a horse, but a whole horse farm. Here was a man bonded to his wife by marriage, children, and religious faith, as well as a $9,000 diamond ring, a $5,000 sapphire cocktail ring, and strings and strings of cultured pearls. Now he and his whole family were dead, money from his business was missing, and so was the diamond ring.

"When rich people are murdered, its almost impossible to separate the issue of their material wealth from the reason for the crime because it so often plays a role," says Wallin.

* * *

On June 8, 1968, a Saturday, Dick and Shirley went out to dinner in Detroit with their closest friends, Roger and Margaret Smith. According to Joe Scolaro, the Smiths were not only the Robisons' close friends, they were their only friends.

"He took a lot of time to make friends and then he cherished them," Joe told detectives. "He would say, 'I have a lot of acquaintances and few friends.' His own family and the Smiths were his only real friends."

Roger Smith was a doctor who worked at Ford Hospital in Detroit, and the couple lived nearby the Robisons in Lathrup Village. The Smith's son, Michael, was Gary Robison's best friend and had spent time at the Good Hart cottage over the past three summer vacations.

The dinner conversation must have been easy and familiar, the four-some enjoying a friendship that spanned more than a decade. Margaret told police that she and Shirley felt comfortable talking about their children and civic affairs, but stayed away from discussing anything as private as marital issues.

"I think this relationship was unique compared to most relationships of this sort in that we didn't discuss personal problems that we might have other than something regarding the children," Margaret Smith said. "For instance, if there had been any problem at all at home as far as Richard was concerned she wouldn't have discussed this with me—we respected each other's privacy."

Some time during dinner, however, the talk turned to Dick's business plans. Dr. Smith told police that Dick was excited about "a large business adventure," though he also got the feeling that Shirley disapproved of it. The family didn't need any more money, Shirley demurred, as they already had "all of the things they needed in life."

According to the Smiths, Dick Robison thought that he was about to strike it rich. "[Dick] said he could not tell the details now but when it was completed, he would not have to worry the rest of his life. He also told the Smiths that he wanted them to enjoy some of his success and do some traveling with them at his expense."

This was the first police knew of an impending business deal of this magnitude, and they decided to investigate the matter further. If Dick commanded a salary of $30,000 or $40,000 a year and he thought he was going to make enough money to be set for life, the mysterious business deal had to be worth upwards of half a million dollars. A huge sum in 1968, an amount that provided detectives with a conceivable motive for murder.

"There was something big coming," Margaret Smith said. "Until it was all settled they were just not talking about it which was perfectly alright with us. Of course, now I wish I would have been a much more nosey individual."

As they widened the circle of their interviews, Stearns and Flis received confirmation from many other sources that Dick was indeed planning something. It wasn't necessarily real, but it was big. In Dick's mind, anyway.

His banker, Frank Joity, said that although Dick rarely discussed his business plans, Dick told him in May that he would be making a large transaction in the near future.

A Robison neighbor, Walter Muellenhagen, told police that he and Dick were working out the details of a new business venture and that Dick had "five big-money backers" to fund their planned enterprise. Muellenhagen first met Dick at a square dance club, and they also rubbed elbows at the Lathrup Village Home Owners Council, of which Muellenhagen was president. Muellenhagen declined to tell police the exact nature of the new business, saying he was afraid that if word got out about it, someone else would steal their idea. Even now, after the reality of the murders had sunk in, he was still considering going forward with their plan.

Dick had access to $50 million in capital, Muellenhagen said, and an additional $50 million was available if they needed it. An unfathomable figure that far surpassed the detective's original estimate. The whole plan was sketched out by Dick on a place mat at a Southfield Howard Johnson's restaurant where Muellenhagen, Dick, and Joe Scolaro met to discuss their idea. Muellenhagen told the police that he kept the place mat for a number of weeks, but had recently burned it in his fireplace.

Dick's father, Ross C. Robison, said that his son talked with him about a mysterious new business on June 15, the day before the whole family was to leave for their Good Hart cottage. Dick told his father that he was "winding up a big deal" and when it was complete, he'd be a "tycoon." The whole family was going to Lexington, Kentucky, to buy a horse farm and then on to Naples, Florida, to buy a beachfront condominium. While they were gone, Dick told his father, an in-ground swimming pool and two guest cottages would be constructed on their Good Hart property. And, Dick hinted, Ross should plan to spend the winter in Florida, just like he always dreamed of.

Before they left him alone with his grief, Ross Robison told the police something else that would nag at them for months: A man by the name of Mr. Roeberts or maybe Mr. Roberts would be traveling with Dick, Shirley, and the kids on their real estate buying trip. Mr. Roberts had his own plane, just like Dick, and he would be flying into the Pellston Airport, would spend a few days at the cottage with the family, and then they would all travel south together.

"When I get back from the trip, I will have something big to tell you," Dick told his father. If the elder Robison needed anything while they were away, Ross was to contact Joe Scolaro.

* * *

On July 24, 1968, petitions were filed in the Oakland County probate court on behalf of the Robison estate's two beneficiaries, Shirley's brother, Marvin Fulton, and Dick's sister, Elaine Fox. Dick and Shirley each had a will, and each had named the other as primary beneficiary. In the event they both died, a trust was to be set up for their four children. The murder of an entire family is not a contingency most people consider when they swear out their will. Eventually, a four-way split of the estate, which turned out to be worth approximately $200,000, was decided between Marvin Fulton, Elaine Fox, Ross Robison, and Shirley's mother, Aileen Fulton. Two hundred thousand dollars was an entirely respectable amount of money in 1968 for the life's work of one man, killed unexpectedly in his early forties, but still a far cry from $100 million.

By the beginning of August, Stearns and Flis had begun the process of sifting through Dick Robison's finances, and though they had gleaned a few useful discoveries within the chaff of paperwork, old files, and cancelled checks, if $100 million were hiding in there anywhere, the detectives had yet to find it. Cal Mackey, who along with his father, Maurice Mackey, had looked after Dick's finances since 1955, said he didn't know anything about an influx of that kind of money into R. C. Robison and Associates, *Impresario*, or the newly formed Impresario Cultural Society.

"[S]ome time in the early part of June, Dick did talk to my dad on the telephone and made the comment that by the first of September we would all be millionaires and that he wouldn't tell anything until the first of September when he came back down from up north," Cal Mackey told the detectives. "To the best of my knowledge, that was the only conversation they had."

"Was this an unusual thing with Dick?" Stearns asked.

"No, Dick Robison was a dreamer," said Mackey.

"But the fact of him getting rich, this wasn't unusual?"

"No."

"Or a big money deal?"

"No."

"He had many of these, I take it, in the past?"

"He had a lot of them he talked about, yes."

"Do you know if there was any discussion as to what this was?"

"All he talked about, basically all his dreams were in regards to the magazine. *Impresario* was a phenomenally strong tool; it could be made to do anything he wanted to do. It could control the world as far as he was concerned. And he intended to build *Impresario* hotels throughout the world. That was his basic dream."

But as far as the money needed to finance Dick's dream, Mackey said he could find no evidence of it.

* * *

In an effort to more fully identify Dick's mysterious tycoon-in-the-making business idea, Stearns interviewed two men that Walter Muellenhagen led them to: Arnold Park and William McKinley, managers of the New Hudson Airport in Oakland County, just outside Detroit.

A few miles west of Lathrup Village, the facility opened in 1946 and first functioned as a place for war veterans to train for their pilot's license courtesy of the G.I. Bill. In the year 2000, Oakland County would buy the airport and its surrounding eighty-three acres of property for $3.6 million in grant money from the State of Michigan's coffers.

In 1968, however, a man named W. S. Nagel owned the facility and Park and McKinley managed it. The airport by then specialized in providing service to the owners of small two- and four-seat airplanes. One of their clients was Dick Robison, and when they arrived at the airport, police found Dick's Sky Hawk safely parked inside a hangar in its regular spot, undisturbed. Stearns, Flis, and Park examined the plane and found nothing amiss, nothing that could help in the investigation. If the Robisons had planned a trip south, and if they had planned to travel by air, it wasn't going to be in this airplane.

Dick did, however have something cooking with Park and McKinley. In the middle of May, about the same time that he had given his banker a heads-up, Dick told the men that he was planning something big and he wanted them to be involved. The detectives had heard all this before, of course, but this time, they had found two men who not only knew the details of Dick's plans, but were willing to talk about them.

For two months, from the middle of April until the middle of June, Dick and Joe Scolaro took a drive around the airport nearly every single day, the men said. During that time, several meetings were held between the four men to discuss Dick's grandiose ideas. Luxury motels, pilot townhouses, a cultural center, international tour planning, visiting artists supported with the profits from large warehouses where a variety of goods could be stored, purchased, and shipped. All of this activity was to be centered within an expanded executive airport terminal and eventually even franchised at other airports throughout the country—this was the dream of Dick Robison. A dream that he planned to make real, in its first physical incarnation at least, at the New Hudson Airport beginning in September 1968. Just as soon as he and his family returned from Summerset.

Park and McKinley would manage the facility, and funding for the project would be provided with investment from five wealthy financiers that Dick said he had already lined up. The financial figure he shared with Park and McKinley was $11.5 million, however, just over a tenth of the $100 million that had been quoted by Muellenhagen. But another part of the men's story had the ring of truth to it. They too knew of the elusive Mr. Roeberts and had even spoken to him on the phone. At least they thought he was the man they had spoken to.

On June 12, Dick came to the airport just as he had been doing nearly every day for the past two months and told the men to expect a phone call that very same day from a man named Mr. Roeberts. Mr. Roeberts wanted to set up appointments with them to work out the specifics of the new airport-centered enterprise. Just before five o'clock, a man calling himself Mr. Roeberts did call. He said that he was calling about the airport project, that he wanted to meet with Park and McKinley, and that he would call back within the week to set something up.

Although the men had been expecting the call, something about it just felt off, they told detectives.

"Mr. Park described an elderly man with a low monotone voice and he had frequent pauses in his speech," detectives wrote in their report. "He stated that it was a very unusual voice and he got the feeling he was talking to some robot."

A few minutes after Arnold Park ended his conversation with this mysterious man with the odd robotic voice, Dick called, and inquired whether they had heard from Mr. Roeberts. Yes, they told him, they had heard from the man; he had called as expected but nothing definite was decided. Dick then gave them the same instructions he'd give his father Ross three days later: he was headed to his cottage in Good Hart, but if they needed anything while he was gone, they could call Joe Scolaro "and he would take care of them."

On June 21, Park said Mr. Roeberts called the airport again, and the conversation was much the same as before. A robotic voice and a promise to call back in a week to schedule appointments.

A check of Dick's home phone records in Lathrup Village revealed the call he made to the airport on June 12 to confirm that Park and McKinley had heard from Mr. Roeberts, but no record of either of the calls made by Roeberts himself. Stearns and Flis didn't know if Mr. Roeberts was the murderer, one of the five investors, or a straw man, invented in a swindle by Dick or Joe or even the two working together. For now, Mr. Roeberts, or Roberts or whatever his name was, was a phantom—a ghost really, who spoke with an inhuman voice and disappeared four days before the murder, almost as if he had never lived.

With few other clues as compelling as this now missing and presumably wealthy ghostlike man, in early August 1968 detectives Stearns and Flis began their search for Mr. Roeberts in earnest. Not surprisingly, their first stop was the doorstep of Joe Scolaro. On August 7 they brought Joe into the Detroit headquarters of the state police at ten in the morning and grilled him until three in the afternoon. They taped their interview with him, gave him a Miranda warning, and then got Joe to agree to voluntarily take the first of three lie detector tests.

The essence of his story was this: Joe said he knew that Dick had big plans for *Impresario* and R. C. Robison and Associates, and thought he had overheard his boss mention a man by the name of Mr. Roeberts. But he didn't know who Mr. Roeberts was, had never seen or met him, and had no idea how detectives could get in contact with this mystery man.

"Who is Mr. Roeberts?" Stearns came right out and asked Joe for the second time.

"Beats the hell out of me," Joe replied, mirroring the answer he gave detectives the first time he was asked. "I personally had a feeling that Mr. Roeberts could have been part of his investors because when he did mention the name to me, we were over at Lansing at the airport. . . . We were talking about the airport deal. I said, 'Boy, that was going to cost a hell of a lot of money. These people must be pretty sharp.' We were talking about an airplane that just came in and then he mentioned the name Mr. Roeberts, and went on about how wonderful these people were and everything, and then he looked at me and said, 'You forget that I said that.'"

"That's funny," Stearns said, when Joe continued to deny that he knew anything specific about the mystery man. "He told his wife about Roeberts, so he didn't plan it to be a secret. He wrote a letter with Roeberts' name in it, stating that he would be up there. Isn't it strange that he wouldn't tell you about Roeberts?"

"No," said Joe. "As I said, he mentioned the name out at the airport and that was it, period. . . . That's why I say I personally feel that maybe

Roeberts could be involved with us, maybe not. Roeberts might be, as far as I am concerned, a fictitious name, I really don't know."

"Don't you think it is rather strange that this Mr. Roeberts, if there was such a person that was supposed to be involved in these deals, hasn't made any contact?" Stearns asked.

"I think it is extremely strange," Joe replied.

With Joe a seeming dead end, police turned their attention elsewhere. They interviewed a colleague of Muellenhagen's named Ellis Jeffers, who Joe had told them came up with the original idea of the warehousing portion of Dick's business plan. Jeffers ran a company in Detroit called Industrial Purchasing Cooperative, and had joined Dick, Joe, and Muellenhagen in an all-day meeting in the spring of 1968 where they discussed the possibility of going into business together. Again, detectives heard that Dick had access to $50 million up front, with another $50 million available later.

Jeffers said he had never heard the name Mr. Roeberts. He never knew where the money for the venture was supposed to come from, but wasn't convinced the funds were legitimate or even real.

"After the meeting, Jeffers was not quite satisfied with the way Robison did business," police noted. "He said he did not see enough on paper and felt that Robison's way of doing things was slipshod."

In the weeks before the murders, Dick and Jeffers had a falling out, and Jeffers said he was pushed out of the deal; if Muellenhagen went ahead with it, Jeffers said he just might get it in his head to sue. He'd already had his lawyer send out a cease-and-desist letter. Jeffers agreed to take a polygraph test and, just like Muellenhagen, passed.

Police then interviewed former employees of Dick's, his attorney, clients of the advertising firm, neighbors of the Robison family, many of their friends and relatives, and even fellow parishioners from their Lutheran church. They contacted border patrol offices as far away as Mexico and Canada. No one had ever heard of Mr. Roeberts or had the slightest inkling of who he could be. But while police didn't uncover this elusive phantom man, they did find something else almost as interesting: the first hard proof of shady business dealings at R. C. Robison and Associates.

The dark stain on Dick's ad firm's reputation began with his biggest client, Delta Faucet, and spread from there. Helen Hoeft, private secretary to Delta executive Harry Ford, told the detectives that her boss was planning to sever his relationship with Dick and hire another advertising firm, mainly because Dick was rarely available when Mr. Ford needed him. He was either at his Good Hart cottage, holed up in a hotel somewhere, or working at home and didn't want to be disturbed. Dick must have known about these rumors himself, she said, because in the weeks before the murder he had begun calling her on the phone and questioning her about this very problem.

"She further advised that in the early part of July 1968, Mr. Joseph Scolaro called the main office in Greensburg, Indiana and asked [company comptroller] Mr. George James to send him an advance because he was having problems operating the business and that there was a shortage of operating money. She stated that she did not know the amount and since that time there is doubt in her mind whether the money had been used for business purposes or for Scolaro's own personal use." Though neither had an exact figure, both Hoeft and James indicated the advance could have been $25,000 or more.

On the last day of March 1969, Stearns and Flis made good use of a state police airplane and its contracted pilot and were flown from Detroit to Greensburg, Indiana, where they got an earful from a few key employees of Delta. Comptroller George James and sales manager Byron Carr told detectives they had seen evidence that Robison's ad firm had been experiencing financial difficulties for the past two or three years. Though Joe Scolaro had only called Delta that one time asking for an advance, Dick had made that same call as many as four times, each time requesting an advance on an invoice, saying he needed the money to keep his business afloat.

Carr then told police that Dick was about to lose his biggest client. In March 1968, another advertising firm had made a presentation to the company, pitching its services. The presentation was well received, and Delta planned to change its ad firm as of January 1, 1969. Robison was on his way out, though Carr could not say for sure if Dick knew this or not. Immediately after the murders, however, Harry Ford had advised George James that he was not to pay any new R. C. Robison and Associates invoices without Ford's express approval. Some of the magazines that Dick had placed Delta's advertisements in had not been paid, even though his firm had already been paid for both the ads and their commission.

There was, detectives learned, a paper trail left behind by the exchange of money between Delta and Dick's firm. Stearns and Flis were given copies of all transactions between Delta and R. C. Robison and Associates for 1968, as well as the originals of seven canceled checks written between April and September from Delta to R. C. Robison and Associates totaling more than $81,000.

The detectives returned to Michigan by plane that same day, making a stop at the East Lansing airport, where an officer from the state police's latent print unit met them on the tarmac and took possession of the files. Check them for Joe Scolaro's fingerprints, Stearns instructed.

* * *

Back on the ground and on the job, detectives continued to look into Dick's finances, increasingly convinced that the seed of murder grew from this fertile ground. They interviewed anyone they could find who had business dealings with Dick and Joe. One of them was a Birmingham advertising salesman, Robert Anderson. Anderson met Dick in the mid-1960s when the two ad men crossed paths at Masco Corporation, Delta's parent company headquartered in Detroit. Anderson interviewed for a job with R. C. Robison and Associates in the fall of 1967 and went to work for Dick in April of 1968. He was still at the firm, he said, now working for Joe, even though he continued to have the feeling that something wasn't right with the company.

"After he started working for the Richard C. Robison Company, he felt that there might have been some false billing by RCR to the Delta Faucet Co. This false billing by RCR consisted of overcharging in very large amounts. . . . Anderson did not have any evidence to show this, but felt a check of the company records may disclose the discrepancies."

Those records were now in the possession of who else but Joe Scolaro. Joe had bought R. C. Robison and Associates company from the Robison estate for just $3,500 a few months after the murders, and so he owned all the company's assets, debts, and financial records, some dating back five years or more.

Detectives wasted no time in confronting Joe with the allegations of overcharging Delta and convinced him to turn over all of the files documenting the company's past and present financial doings. Under threat of a subpoena, he did. The National Bank of Detroit was also contacted, and turned over copies of all of its records having to do with the bank accounts of R. C. Robison and Associates.

When detectives surveyed the jumble of paperwork piled high and now spanning eight years, from 1960 to 1968, they must have felt as if they were locked in a room packed with straw that they had to spin into gold. They needed a Rumpelstiltskin—or at least a good accountant. They found their magic in a rather unlikely place, the Oakland County Prosecutor's Office.

On April 15, Stearns and Flis contacted Oakland County assistant prosecutor John Bain, updated him on the investigation, told him they suspected financial misdeeds by Dick Robison, Joe Scolaro, or both, and asked that he assign an accountant at county expense to the case, someone who could find a motive in all that money. They were in luck. Eugene Freedman, who worked as an assistant prosecutor for the county, happened to have spent several years as an agent for the Internal Revenue Service before he became a prosecutor. Freedman, Bain said, was their man. It was just a co-incidence that they hooked up with the former taxman on tax day.

Freedman, accompanied by Stearns and Flis, spent April 23 in Dick's old office on Southfield Street in Southfield with Joe Scolaro and Dick's former accountant, Cal Mackey, organizing, packing up, and giving a cursory examination to the company's financials. For the next two days, Freedman examined every dollar the company made, spent, billed for, and recorded from 1960 to 1968 and he did indeed spin straw into gold. "Substantial discrepancies" were found, police said. The overcharges on contracted advertising amounted to $3,000 in 1965, $6,000, in 1966, $13,000 in 1967, and $27,000 in the first half of 1968, January through August. The records also revealed that certain ads that were paid for were never run, bringing the total Delta had been bilked to more than $100,000.

"Somebody got caught with their hands in the till," an article published in the *Detroit Free Press* quoted an unnamed detective as saying. This was certainly a veiled reference to Joe.

While detectives were conducting their interviews and the accountant completing his report on the finances, the latent print unit was doing its work, too. It took a month, but on May 1, 1969, detectives found out that the lab had gotten a hit. Four of the seven checks from Delta Faucet Company to R. C. Robison and Associates had Joe Scolaro's fingerprints on them: checks dated April 10, 1968 for $13,156.50; June 10, 1968, for $12,060.76; June 27, 1968, for $6,399.40; and September 5, 1968, for $4,541.41. The total was $36,158.07, of which $10,940.81 had been handled by Joe after the Robisons were dead.

* * *

A few weeks later, Robert Anderson, the sales agent who worked first for Dick and then for Joe, showed up unexpectedly at the Detroit police post and told detectives that if they ever needed to interview him again, they'd have to call him in Chicago. He'd just quit his job with Joe and was moving his family away from the area immediately. He would not, he said, ever again return to his Birmingham home.

"He states that he is afraid of Joseph Scolaro and is in fear of harm to himself and family. He relates that Scolaro is a liar and a cheat and he believes him to have a mental problem. Scolaro has been passing bad checks and the company is in bad financial trouble. He thinks Scolaro has something to do with the Robison family death but was unable to supply officers with anything that would aid in solving the crime."

On Friday, September 12, 1969, at 5:00 p.m., Joseph R. Scolaro was arrested by Detectives Stearns and Flis. The charge was not six counts of first degree murder, but rather obtaining money under false pretenses. After detectives had been hearing figures like $100 million and $50 million tossed around for months, it was just $1,697 that put Joe in front of a judge, an irony that could not have been entirely lost on the detectives.

That is the amount of the bad check Joe wrote against an account he had at the National Bank of Detroit. According to bank records, Joe wrote the check on August 14 against an account with a balance of just $30. He then deposited the check into the R. C. Robison and Associates account. According to police records, the owner of Planned Auto Management leased two cars to Joe on August 15 for a payment of $1,170.26. Joe wrote PAM owner Louis Corsi a check, which bounced. When Corsi confronted him about it, Joe wrote him another check for the same amount from another account with the National Bank of Detroit. This check also bounced. Likely, this was the beginning of the transaction that landed Joe in jail overnight.

The only other interaction Corsi had with Joe was in June 1968. Joe had dropped off one of his cars, a station wagon, for repairs on June 20. Corsi had given him a loaner to use until the repairs were completed. A few days later, he said he tried to contact Joe at work to tell him that his car was ready, but was told by whoever answered the phone that Joe was up north.

When Joe was escorted into the police post, he thought he was being arrested for the murders. Whether this was because of an erroneous assumption he made himself, or a calculated move on the part of detectives isn't clear, but for the next five hours, Stearns and Flis went at him hard. It wasn't until Joe's mother, Kitty, got her son an attorney that he knew the nature of the exact charges against him.

"What am I charged with?" Joe asked Stearns and Flis after the lawyer called the police post and the two spoke on the phone.

"Bad checks," they answered.

That was the end of that interview, and the check kiting charge was eventually dropped. Joe would tell his brother-in-law, Herbert Johnson about it later, sure that the other man had seen the articles reporting his arrest in the Detroit newspapers.

"You know what I did, Herb?" Joe asked.

"No, what did you do?" Johnson responded.

"Well, they call it check kiting," said Joe.

"What the hell does that mean?" asked Johnson.

"Well, that's when you got a bank account here and a bank account here and you're . . . you know," Joe said.

Though detectives didn't get a confession, they did have a better idea of the way Joe dealt with money—he got it any way he could. In an effort to find out whether Joe had used underhanded means to get any of Dick's money, they reinterviewed accountant Cal Mackey.

Mackey explained that while Dick handled the day-to-day expenditures and petty cash, his accounting firm was in charge of payables and payroll. Every two weeks Mackey would get a call from Dick; he'd go to the R. C. Robison and Associates offices and pay the bills and make out the paychecks. If Dick were considering making a large purchase, he would call Mackey and ask him if his company could afford it. If he wanted to give an employee a raise, he would call Mackey and give him a heads-up. That was the protocol from the early 1960s until the first of May 1968. After that, everything changed, and Mackey said he had no idea why.

"Do you have any idea why you weren't called to make any payroll checks or do any accounting after May 1?" Stearns asked Mackey.

"No," Mackey said. "All I know is that every time we did call him or try to contact him he wasn't in the office. He wasn't in the office at all as far as we know. From roughly the first of May on."

"All right, in the past any time that he was going to have any expenditures . . . did you usually know about these ahead of time?"

"We knew about everything ahead of time. If he gave an employee a ten dollar raise either he would call us and ask us if he could afford to give it, number one, and if nothing else what the deduction would be on the check, so we always knew about a raise or anything like that in advance. When he bought his plane he wanted to know if he could afford to buy the plane. There was a case a year before that he wanted to build a sauna bath next to the building. He had called us and asked if he could afford that. So, normally anything he spent any kind of money on, he would call and ask first."

"Is it safe to say that he always checked with you before all raises?"

"My office, right."

After more questioning, Mackey revealed that when Joe went from commission-based pay to a regular salary in early 1968, he was making $10,000 a year, and had a $4,000 annual allowance for expenses, as well as a company car, a compensation package that worked out to just over $1,100 a month. Then at the beginning of May, about the same time that Dick was unavailable to go over the company accounts with Mackey, Joe got a substantial raise.

"Do you have the dates and the figures on that?" Stearns asked.

"On May 9th, he drew the check for $1,500 which was the middle of the month check, which was not a normal period of time. Five days later he drew a check for his normal wages and in the end of May he took a check for $800 which was approximately double what it normally was, and in the month of June he increased his pay to $2,000 per semi-monthly pay period."

"What about expenses during this period?" Stearns asked.

"The amounts run anywhere from five to six hundred dollars in expenses. At a period of time he took roughly $1,500 worth of expense checks," said Mackey.

"Now the period of time we're talking about is between May 1 and . . ."

"June 25th," said Mackey.

"What percent increase would this be, roughly? Two hundred and fifty percent?" Stearns asked.

"If there was an increase. A raise of this type is ridiculous. [Dick] could nowhere in a million years afford this type of a raise on his billings at that time."

"How about the other employees?"

"Well, they got raises, but nowhere near the raise he got."

"Did Dick discuss these raises with you?"

"No sir."

"Did you question anyone on these raises?"

"Not till I learned about them, which was after the date of death. Until then, I knew of no raises whatsoever."

"This was a nearly three month period here then that you weren't called upon to take care of the accounting."

"That's right."

"Do you know from your own personal knowledge who handled the checks?"

"It would appear from the checks that were written and the check stubs that Joseph Scolaro prepared the checks."

"Remember one time we were talking with you here Cal, and you were telling me about you and Dick discussing Joe as a possible signer, or leaving checks with Joe, I believe in the early part of '68?"

"In the early part of '68 Dick Robison and I had a discussion and Dick informed me that he wanted Joe to have nothing to do with the checkbook at all. That it wasn't a book that he was supposed to be in and he wanted his nose kept out of it. Just that simple. He told me if Joe asked any questions about it, just tell him that it was none of his business."

"All right, the bodies were discovered on July the 22, 1968. Can you give me a rough estimate as to the amount of money that Joe Scolaro received, wages and expense accounts, between June 25 and July 22?"

"It would be $8,000," said Mackey.

"$8,000."

"Right."

"All right," Stearns asked, "after May 1 were there any check stubs there where Dick's handwriting appeared on checks written to Joe?"

"No," answered Mackey.

"Is it safe in assuming then that all checks that were wrote to Joe Scolaro after May 1 were probably wrote by him?" asked Stearns.

"They were either written by him or typed," answered Mackey.

Another detail at least as important as the activity on the company checkbook came to light during the interview with Joe. While they had him in custody, Stearns and Flis took the opportunity to question him yet again about the murders. Joe gave them the same story about his comings and goings on the day of the murders and the same story about the purchase of the Berettas. But the interview wasn't a total bust. Joe also told detectives something new.

Some time in the mid-1960s, Joe said, he bought two Armalite .22-caliber model AR-7 Explorer survival rifles. He bought them from his gun dealer brother-in-law, Herbert Johnson, of Pontiac. Joe couldn't produce the rifles for police though, saying he gave one of them to a friend and gave the other one back to his brother-in-law.

The phone call from the lawyer his mother had hired came in before the detectives could press him further, but finding Joe's AR-7s became a top priority before their suspect had even left the room.

The Tipsters

1969

Dear Sir, I am no crank. Please check this story out to the finish . . . I know who killed that family.

> —Anonymous letter addressed to the director of the FBI, dated October 4, 1972

A year went by and the crime was still unsolved despite numerous tips received by police, both signed and anonymous. Now a thickening stew of collective fear, moral outrage, civic duty, personal problems, and honest—if morbid—curiosity inspired an additional assortment of tipsters to bring their knowledge, real or imagined, to bear on the investigation. The $5,000 reward put up by the *Detroit News* didn't hurt any, either.

In the 1960s the *News* had initiated a secret witness program designed to solve serious but baffling crimes by protecting the identity of informants. The theory was that for every unsolved crime that had stymied law enforcement, at least one anonymous person knew who the perpetrator was and might come forward if promised two things: secrecy and money.

The newspaper put aside $100,000 of reward money to be used in the program and, after some early successes, gained the blessing of many city cops, state police, and county sheriff's departments. After a request from both Commissioner Frederick Davids of the Michigan State Police and Sheriff Richard Zink of Emmet County, the *News* bent its rule that all crimes in the program had to have occurred in the Detroit area, and the Robison murder case was featured in an August 11 secret witness article.

"Under the 'secret witness' program the informant may supply data which—without his name—is turned over to law enforcement agencies," the article explained. "If conviction results, the reward is paid in similar secrecy."

The *News* directed responders to write a letter detailing their knowledge of the crime and to sign it, not with their given name but rather with a six-digit number of their own choosing. The same six-digit number was to be written on a corner of the letter, torn off before mailing, and kept by the tipster. In the event their tip led to a conviction, the torn corner with their number written on it would be proof of their valid claim for the reward money.

Responses came in to the newspaper's office then, but many were from correspondents who, despite their assurances to the contrary, came across to law enforcement as cranks, busybodies, or outright psychotics. One informant wrote that he had information to give, but that in order to get it, law enforcement officials had to place the following classified ad in the *News'* personals section: "Dr. Guidini: Your prescription good. However, need additional. Zodius."

The ad was placed once in September 1968 and again in January 1969, and mentioned in a news article under the headline, "Is Key to Robisons' Killer in Classified Ad?" There was no response, and as far as anyone knows, the informant was never heard from again. The nature of the "prescription" and the identity of "Dr Guidini" and "Zodius" remain unfathomable.

Some responders forgot to put a number on their tip, while still others, it seemed, cared not for the ability to protect their identity, they just wanted the money. Some, officers must have thought, were just plain deranged.

"I am a patient at Hawthornden St. Hospital. I am perfectly sane and I do a lot of research work," began one letter to Sheriff Zink. Another stated, "I am not a nut or a prankster, but I do have E.S.P."

One man wrote of the suspicious actions of his neighbor, saying the man quit his job at the Chevy plant in Flint, moved to Atlanta, went broke, moved back to Flint, couldn't find another job, and "ran to this place and that place." He was seen cleaning his gun right before leaving on a hunting trip to Petoskey in early June, so surely he was the murderer.

Another man by the name of Charles McReynolds signed his name to his tip and gave himself number 125115. He wrote that a cellmate of his from Milan Correctional Institute was now living in Detroit and was the owner of a pool hall on Jefferson Street and a factory on Lafayette Street. This man was making bombs for the government in his factory, using his partner's name to get government contracts. The tipster had already received a reward from Lloyds of London for helping solve a jewelry heist, so he knew the drill. "If talking to me," the letter advised, "please be careful."

If detectives had not yet marveled at the preponderance of oddballs with some imaginary connection to this case, they could hardly have avoided that thought after receiving a strange letter in June 1971. "Look back 40 years in the Robison family. They has [*sic*] a deep dark secret," the writer advised. "The night the Robison family was kill [*sic*] in that cabin I seen it and heard it because it wake me up. I could not go back to sleep. I told my family that lots of people got kill not so far from here. . . . I told them what the mens [*sic*] look like I see them in the spirit. . . he is Robison own son the hate came from his mother she taught the boy all of that hate it is so bad."

The letter was handwritten in large cursive script, six pages long, though the pages were marked with the letters A through F instead of being numbered. The writer also described in detail the clothing of the two killers: one was wearing a two-piece corduroy outfit with a cap that had flaps covering his ears, and red socks that covered the top of his boots, which were laced up with buckskin strings. The other had on a dark suit with an overcoat, was bareheaded and wore horn-rimmed glasses. The letter was signed, "Queen Esther Best."

Medicine doctors, strange Greek god–sounding names, a queen, and a pool-shooting bomb-maker. While the newspaper's secret witness program didn't net anything of real value, state police detectives continued to receive tips from citizens directly, who called them on the phone, wrote letters, or approached police in person.

A driver headed north turned in a hitchhiker simply because he was wearing a military jacket; officers learned he was AWOL and just returning to his National Guard unit.

A Lansing woman and mother of four turned in her husband who she said had spent days unaccounted for up north during the approximate time of the murders. He turned out to have been perch fishing on the other side of the state.

A Petoskey mechanic turned in a customer who, he said, "has a lot of guns, a hot temper [and] wrote a story on murder." When the mechanic's tip was checked out, detectives learned that the man's guns had been sold years ago and the story he'd written was an unfinished autobiography about his childhood in Detroit during the depression. The hot temper alone certainly was no crime.

A farmer in Kalkaska turned in his hired hand because the man and his wife got drunk on a workday, and argued about the nature of the work to be done. The woman told the farmer that her husband could "wipe out your whole family." The couple left the farm after the outburst and had not returned.

A friend turned in his drinking buddy because he had bragged about buying a $400 ring for his girlfriend and the friend wondered how his buddy could have come by that much money.

Another friend turned in his drinking buddy for the same reason, but this time it was a $2,000 bankroll that was in question.

An escapee from Pelston Prison Camp told the state trooper who captured him that he and a ragtag bunch of other inmates would regularly slip out of the prison camp, drive the camp truck to a local bar, buy beer, drink it, and then return to camp. When interviewed, prison staff denied the inmate's account.

The Michigan State Police were not the only beneficiaries of this questionable citizen involvement, however. The Petoskey Police Department got its share of tips, too, as did the Emmet County sheriff. In August 1970 for example, officers there received a letter from a woman named Sophia Bock, a seventy-five-year-old widow living in Detroit. Not only did she know who committed the Robison murders, the letter said, she had information on three other unsolved homicides as well. It was her neighbors, the Williams family, who did the deeds. Next door, she said, lived people "at the center of the ring of murdering and theft murderers." When officers visited with Mrs. Bock, however, they learned she was more suspicious of her neighbor's race than anything else. Mrs. Bock, who was white, was afraid to live next door to a black family.

"In the Robison murder, she knew that they had committed it because they bought a car at about that time, but could elaborate no further," detectives noted in their report. "She gave various other reasons for the other murders, such as the woman got a wig at the time or somebody came and knocked at their door at two o'clock in the morning, etc. It was obvious to officers that her mind is failing her. She had nothing to aid in this investigation."

These were all Michigan-based tips, but some came to detectives from across state lines, too. Sometimes, these tips from other states seemed to grow in intricacy the further away they originated.

A Pensacola, Florida, minister named Erskine Belk wrote to state police captain Guy Babcock, who was stationed in Traverse City, expressing his interest in the case and hinting at the possibility that he had some relevant information. What he wanted, he said, was an update on the investigation. "I may be able to furnish you with a lead," Belk said in his letter, "then again, what information I have may not be of any use at all. But if you will write, I'll be glad to do what I can."

Belk's letter was passed along to Captain Raymond McConnell at the East Lansing post, who updated him by first-class mail on the generalities of the investigation. Belk wrote back, giving the names of "a man and his wife and about four children living here that everything does not seem 'just right.'"

The family's name was Hayes and they had left Flint and moved to Pensacola without benefit of a job, a place to live, adequate funds, or even proper luggage, but just came south willy-nilly in a Cadillac convertible with their belongings stuffed in paper bags. They slept in their car or under picnic tables on the beach, the parents taking odd jobs during the day. Such a haphazard life, undertaken by choice, the reverend could not abide.

"His wife works as a book keeper. His children seem real nice and appear to have been outstanding students at the school they attended in Flint. All appear to be normal except him, or maybe he is and I'm just a suspicious old man!" Belk wrote in his second letter to the state police.

McConnell found that the man in question, one Hazelip Winston Hayes, was the bearer of a revoked Michigan driver's license, having been arrested many times in Flint for drunk driving and various traffic violations, causing him to be a "frequent guest of the Flint Police Dept." McConnell could also document eight addresses for the family in the past three years. Mr. Hayes was not, however, the murderer of the Robisons, nor a fugitive from any other form of justice—unless that justice was simply your run-of-the-mill adult responsibility.

Northern Michigan locals didn't escape suspicion, either, even when they had worked on the investigation. An anonymous correspondent wrote a handwritten letter to attorney general Frank J. Kelley warning that undersheriff Clifford Fosmore "started buying a lot of excavating machines" after the murder. "The way I know Clifford Fosmore owned all of those excavating machines was because and is a matter of fact because the late Clifford Fosmore had both his first name and his last name on all of his excavating machines that he bought."

The correspondent stated that the source of his information was his father, who also worked as an excavator in the area. His father, whom the writer declined to name, didn't write to Mr. Kelley himself because he didn't want to cause trouble. The writer thought that "this information might lead up to catching the killer or killers . . . who originally lived in Detroit, Michigan."

Fosmore had been hired by the Robison estate to dispose of the cottage, and there were some discrepancies about where certain valuables were located. "Attempts have been made to check out the possibilities of a larceny from the cottage with the Emmet County Undersheriff, Clifford Fosmore but the integrity of the Undersheriff can be questioned for the reliability of any statements he makes," detectives wrote to their captain, Guy Babcock, in a September 15, 1969, memo.

There was no love lost between the state police and Undersheriff Fosmore, at the beginning of the investigation at least. Still, the disorganized tone of the anonymous letter accusing him, the lack of proof of any wrongdoing, and the chance that the writer's father was a competitor of Fosmore's who may have even bid against Fosmore on contracts, made the claims highly suspect. As did the anonymous nature of the tip.

"Please use all the information above this paragraph and the information on the other side of the letter to investigate again the Richard C. Robison families [*sic*] murders, but please keep all of my handwriting strictly confidential and definitely from the press," the writer noted.

In November 1970, however, detectives learned something that rang true, though where exactly it fit in determining a motive for the crime, they couldn't be certain.

On November 9 a young man named Karl Olbrich called the Second District headquarters in Detroit and said that if some officers were willing to come to his Wallace Street home in Birmingham, he and three of his friends might have some valuable information to share. Detectives knew by Olbrich's street address that he was a neighbor of Joe Scolaro's, and they set up a meeting with him and his friends the very next evening.

Five men attended this meeting: Detective Lloyd Stearns, the caller Karl Olbrich and his half-brother George Boehnke, George's relative and roommate Werner Boehnke, and their mutual friend, Timothy Duff. The meeting took place at the Boehnke's Henrietta Street home in Birmingham, several blocks from the sightline of Joe Scolaro.

As background, Karl, a native of Germany, said that he had been friends with Joe for several years, the two sharing an interest in trap shooting. Karl and Joe went target shooting together regularly, and Karl related that he and Joe had gone target shooting with Joe's AR-7. Karl was intrigued by the gun, and took it to show George, who happened to be home on leave from the army. George said he had seen a gun just like it while serving in Germany, and was surprised to learn it was also available to civilians.

Then the men got down to business. The reason Karl called the police post, he told Stearns, was that in June 1968, Joe made an odd request. If Karl would make a phone call, Joe would pay him ten dollars. Karl agreed, walked across the street to Joe's house, and the pair went down to use the phone in the basement. Joe told Karl that he had been working on a big deal at work and that one of the other employees working on the deal had just quit. Joe needed somebody to make a phone call pretending to be that employee.

Karl told Stearns he didn't really understand what Joe was talking about, but agreed to make the call anyway. Joe wrote down what Karl was supposed to say and asked him to read it out loud a couple times before he placed the call. Karl practiced his lines several times, but Joe was unhappy with his German accent. Karl called George, who came over a few minutes later with their friend, Timothy Duff. George tried to read the note, but he too had a German accent. Finally, Duff tried, passed muster with Joe, and agreed to make the call and speak the required lines.

All four men remembered that Timothy was calling Mr. Robison, though none of them remembered whom he was supposed to be impersonating. Joe dialed the phone and handed the receiver to Duff. A young girl answered and Duff asked for Mr. Robison. Joe had warned Duff not to carry on a conversation with Mr. Robison; if Robison asked any questions, Duff was to tell him to contact "Mr. Scolaro."

"None of them could recall just what the content of the note was but it went something like the following," Stearns wrote in his report. "I'm calling in regards to the deal we have been working on with Mr. Scolaro and my client has informed me that he will go as much as five but no more. If you want any more of the details contact Mr. Scolaro as he has the complete package."

After they left Joe's, the men talked among themselves about the incident, wondering if the word "five" in the phone script meant $500, $5,000, or even $5 million.

Back at the police post, Detective Stearns checked the military records of George Boehnke and the phone records from Joe's home phone on Wallace Street. George was on leave from March 16 to April 15, 1968, which was when he saw Joe's AR-7, confirming that Joe had possession of such a gun two months before the murders. Joe's home phone records showed that two calls were made from his house to the Robison cottage in Good Hart on June 24, 1968; one at 8:22 p.m. lasting nine minutes and the other at 8:42 p.m. lasting less than a minute.

During Stearns's interview with the men, Duff said that Dick Robison had sounded quite pleased with the news Duff had just delivered over the phone. Maybe it was $5 million, Duff mused. That would sure put a smile on most men's faces. Less than twenty-four hours later, Stearns knew, Dick and his family were dead.

A Leg Man

1968

He had a tremendous fixation and
fascination of other women--Dick
was strange.

—Joseph R. Scolaro, quoted during his second
polygraph examination, October 18, 1968

Dick was hard on secretaries the way some businessmen are hard on dress shoes—he scuffed them up, wore them out, and broke through their weak parts. These women either bent to his will or, crying and clutching at their clothes, ran out on him, the screen door, office door, or hotel room door slamming shut in their wake.

His secretaries had names like Gail, Helen, Belinda, Wanda, Corrine, Bonnie, and Glenda, and Dick went through all seven of these and unknown others in his ten years in the advertising business. Young, pretty, and polite, these were women fresh from high school graduations or secretarial school training, most of them with plans to work for a few years and then get married and start a family.

The chronology went like this: Wanda (Hensley) Britt worked for Dick from 1963 to 1965; Gail Cornforth Barnes from April 1, 1965, to September 1966; Gwendolyn Syke from July 1966 to September 1966; Bonnie Jean Srull from January 1967 to September 1967; Corrine (Newton) Loop from some time in 1966 to September 1967; and Glenda Sutherland from September 1967 until the murders were discovered in July 1968.

The last in this beleaguered line was just twenty-two years old when her boss was murdered, and she had worked for him for less than a year. Glenda must have been competent, though, because when Joe Scolaro bought the business from the Robison estate in October, she stayed on as his secretary, maintaining her salary of $510 a month, a generous sum at the time for secretarial work.

Detectives Lloyd Stearns and Lewis Wilson interviewed Glenda for just twenty minutes at the R. C. Robison and Associates office the day after the bodies were discovered, along with most of Robison's other employees, including production manager Leo Sawchuck. Sawchuck told detectives Dick Robison was "a man of strong principles and violent temper but was easy to work for if you understood him."

Glenda either understood him or maybe just tolerated his temper to keep her job, because in their report of that initial interview detectives wrote, "She described Mr. Robison the same as Mr. Sawchuck had, and could add nothing further to assist in the investigation."

Stearns and Wilson had no reason to suspect that Glenda was leaving out anything important; the other five Robison employees they interviewed that day had characterized their boss in exactly this same way. He was odd, with a tendency toward angry outbursts, but still they considered him to be an employer who provided interesting work and paid well.

Then, during the state police's second polygraph examination of Joe Scolaro, Joe revealed some interesting information, confirming the detectives' long-held suspicions about Dick's relationships, or desired relationships, with the women who worked for him. There was a pretty good chance that those relationships had gone well beyond a straightforward business arrangement, Scolaro said. Right before his death, Joe suggested, such behavior by Dick was about to become even more frequent.

"I felt that at that point he was getting a mistress," Joe said to polygraph examiner E. Goss. "A secretary mistress. He was being supplied like anybody in the advertising business could supply a girl in a strange town or something like that."

According to Joe, Dick chased his secretaries and was also enamored with a beautiful but married blonde he met in a Detroit art club. But he was most excited about the secretary he said his new investors would be providing to "meet his every want and need."

A woman named Joyce Shores, a beauty, was coming to work for him, Dick told Joe, and she was so beguiling that Joe was going to have a hard time keeping his mind on work. In one of the many loose ends of this case, detectives never found any sign of Ms. Shores. They checked all the local and national associations of secretaries, the state police files, and the Michigan Secretary of State files. Nothing. No sign of anyone by that name.

Dick had also been attracted to a local artist, and that was one of the reasons he had been thinking of renting a studio, according to Joe.

"I know that he was very, very attracted to a gal down at the Scarab Club which is an artist club where he was going to take a studio," Joe told detectives. "And Dick was going to take a studio down there, you know, so he could get away and all that. And he met this gal and all he told me was, before things get completely out of hand he said, 'I'm not going to take the studio. That's all I would need is to have Shirley come in there sometime.'"

Detectives considered whether Dick's behavior with young women could be a motive for murder. Was their seemingly passive victim really a wolf who looked good in a business suit? Detectives decided to reinterview Glenda Sutherland, but this time they would call her into the police post, away from the prying eyes of her coworkers, and ask some personal and maybe even awkward questions. By now, the investigation was growing colder, and they didn't even have a surefire motive for the crime. The time for politeness, if there ever was such a time, was over.

Their simple idea for a more private and serious-minded interview with the young woman worked, and though this pair of seen-it-all detectives could not have predicted what Dick's former secretary would tell them, they were ready to listen. With the passage of time and in this more private setting, Glenda was plenty forthcoming.

It all started, she said, when Dick asked her to stay at work past five one day. After that first time, she knew what to expect. Dick would invite her into his office and lock the door. She would stand in the middle of the room and Dick would ask her to hold her dress up around her waist so that he could look at her legs. He would stare at her legs for what seemed to Glenda like a very long time, and then finally he would run his hands over them. He didn't kiss her, he didn't touch her anywhere else, and he didn't ask her to take off her clothes.

"He told me that he just got his satisfaction out of looking at me and touching my legs," Glenda told the detectives.

Ten times in her ten months of employment Dick engaged in this strange behavior with Glenda, each locked-door "session" lasting as long as an hour. Dick told Glenda he had more elaborate plans for the two of them, though he was murdered before any of them were acted on. The young secretary told Stearns and Flis that Dick wanted her to go with him on business trips where they would stay together in the same hotel room and take off all of their clothes. He said he did not plan to kiss her and they would not engage in sex, but someday he wanted to paint a nude portrait of her.

Before the interview was over, Stearns and Flis asked Glenda to write down the names and contact information for each of Dick's former secretaries and other female employees, which she did without complaint. Detectives were pretty certain that Glenda had not been the only young, unsuspecting woman to hear the click of Dick's office door.

As it turned out, she wasn't. On Glenda's list were almost a dozen names, though the only ones detectives were able to track down and inter-view were Bonnie Jean Srull, twenty-six, Corrine Loop, age unknown, Gail Barnes, twenty-six, Gwendolyn Syke, age unknown, and Wanda Hensley, thirty-five.

The detectives' first visit was to Gail Barnes, from Sterling Heights. Gail was Dick's secretary from April 1965 to September 1966. She came close to confirming their suspicion that their victim was a serial sexual ha-rasser, but stopped just short. Yes, she had been on business trips with Dick, sometimes flying to distant cities in his private plane just for lunch and then returning to Detroit the same afternoon, and yes, she had been asked by him to stay in the office after hours, but all they did together was talk. Nothing untoward ever happened between them, she said.

"Since leaving the Robison employment Mrs. Barnes has married and is about to have a child, and it is this officer's opinion that Mrs. Barnes is re-luctant to relate any experiences she may have encountered with Mr. Robi-son," Stearns wrote in his report. "She did, however, advise that she heard remarks that Robison had some type of an affair with an ex-secretary by the name of Wanda."

Detectives had already heard from several sources—Ernest Gilbert, managing editor, of *Impresario* had told them about it and so had art direc-tor, Richard Stockwell—that Dick and Wanda had engaged in a full-blown affair. They also learned she had married "well" and moved to Florida. Hearing it from yet another source made them more certain than ever that they wanted to speak with Wanda Hensley.

Before securing permission to make the trip all the way to Palm Beach Shores, Florida, the detectives met with Bonnie Jean Srull, art director of Robison's *Impresario* magazine in 1966 and 1967. Like Gail, Bonnie lived in Sterling Heights, had married after she left Robison's employ, and was also pregnant with her first child.

When they met with her, they found another woman willing to talk about the predilections of Dick Robison. Three months after Dick hired her, Bonnie said, he started acting squirrelly. He suggested they become more than just employer and employee, but she told him, "No dice." Dick was nothing if not persistent, however, and tried a few more times to inter-est her in some form of physical relationship. She rebuffed him again. Then in August 1967, when Dick returned home after spending a few summer weeks in Good Hart, he called his office and asked Bonnie to come to his house and bring along the projects she'd been working on. He was working at home, he said, and didn't want to get tied up with office phone calls and correspondence. His working-at-home schedule and odd behavior, Joe told Stearns, was a way for Dick to emulate his idol, Howard Hughes.

Bonnie told the detectives that against her better judgment, she did go to his house, but that, as she feared, what transpired could not be called work. Stearns and Flis documented her story in their report of May 8, 1969.

"He instructed her to come to the back door and walk in. She went to the house and walked in and at this time RCR was in another room. He told her to make herself at home in the living room. She said she sat on the couch and a short time later RCR came back, wearing a smoking jacket and nothing but briefs below. He started to advance to her and she took her things and ran out of the house."

When Bonnie got back to the office, the phone rang. It was Dick, asking this time for his secretary, Corrine Loop. It was her turn to bring some papers by his house, and she was to come over immediately. Corrine complied, but came back to the office minutes later in tears, Bonnie said. Both women quit their jobs at R. C. Robison and Associates within the month.

It was time, detectives decided, to take a closer look at the relationship between Wanda Hensley and Dick Robison. Dick's pursuit of his other, younger secretaries was reprehensible and just plain weird, but also appeared to be short-lived. While sleazy, it was not a plausible motive for the murder of an entire family. The rumors about his relationship with Wanda, however, pointed to an intimacy that possibly went beyond mere office shenanigans, and onto something deeper.

Wanda was single when she worked for Dick, and thirty-five years old, making her much older than the other secretaries, and presumably more experienced in handling male attention—both the kind that she invited and the kind that she didn't. Wanda had lasted as Dick's personal secretary for two years, from 1963 until 1965, which was twice as long as most of the other women. By the time detectives caught up with her, she was Wanda Britt, married to a wealthy Ohio industrialist thirty-five years her senior, Raymond E. Britt.

Did Mr. Britt know about the rumors of the affair between his young wife and her boss before she and Britt were married? Was he the jealous type? Did he know Dick Robison or the Robison family? These were the kinds of questions that needed answers, and so in their investigation of Wanda, Detectives Stearns and Flis started with her rich husband.

Working with the Intelligence Division of the Cleveland Police Department, detectives learned that Raymond Britt was founder, president, and chairman of the board of Central States Industrial Sales Company, a manufacturer and distributor of rubber products. Britt founded the company in 1949 after working for Goodyear Rubber for eight years. By the time detectives were investigating him, Central States Industrial Sales was listed high with Dunn & Bradstreet and he had founded another company, Goodwin Golf Grip, which manufactured handle grips for golf clubs. He was seventy years old now, slowing down a bit, and though he and Wanda had a house in Cleveland, they spent most of their time at their house in southern Florida.

Britt had no criminal record, just an arrest for drunk and disorderly when he was in his thirties, but where his personal finances were concerned, he did have a reputation for being a bit of a high roller—as well as for being intensely jealous of anyone who paid attention to his much-younger wife. Detectives learned from their Cleveland police contact that in the spring or summer of 1968, Wanda Britt became pregnant. They couldn't imagine that a seventy-year-old man would want a new baby in the house, and they wondered whether Raymond was the true father. In their report, Detectives Stearns and Flis suggested otherwise. Could the father instead be Dick Robison? Was there some blackmail scheme between Dick and Raymond to cover up paternity in exchange for investing in R. C. Robison and Associates? Detectives didn't discount the idea; they had already considered theories more far-fetched than this one.

"In recent years, Britt has invested large sums of money in several other companies," the detectives wrote. "He is reported to be very wealthy and has been known to buy amounts of 50,000 shares in a company at one time. . . . Mr. Britt may have been the money source from which Mr. Robison had been talking about."

In October 1969, Stearns and Flis went to Palm Beach Shores, Florida, to pay Wanda Britt a personal visit. Sixty-five miles north of Miami and five miles north of Palm Beach, the exclusive town of Palm Beach Shores is at the southern tip of Singer Island, which was named in the 1940s for Paris Singer, heir to a sewing machine fortune. Among the approximately nine hundred residents of the Oceanside town, the Britts had some rather noteworthy neighbors.

The developer of the community was A. O. Edwards, the Englishman behind London's famed Savoy and Mayfair hotels. Financier John MacArther, at one time the second richest man in the United States, ran his company for a time from the coffee shop in the local Colonnades Hotel. And, during the John F. Kennedy administration, a bomb shelter was built on the island to protect the president in the event a nuclear strike should hit the Sunshine State while he vacationed at his family compound in Palm Beach.

As long as they were going to be in southern Florida anyway, Detectives also arranged to interview Virgil Wheaton, an artist whose studio had been featured in *Impresario,* and who occasionally wrote articles herself for the magazine. She was sixty-five years old and semiretired, but at one time had socialized with Dick and the rest of the magazine staff. Virgil lived in Riviera Beach, a short drive over a bridge to the Florida mainland from Palm Beach Shores. The detectives met with her on October 8, the day before they were to meet with Wanda Britt.

Virgil told the officers that back in Michigan she had stuck her neck out for Dick, hosting a party for him and inviting all of her swanky contacts in the Detroit art community, thinking the introductions would be useful to both his magazine and his plans to found a new cultural society. The party, however, did not go quite as planned. "Robison became involved with many of them in an argument and was running down all of their art work," the detectives learned. "She described him as a very egotistical person and a tyrant to his help and anyone else that was against what he believed in."

What could Wanda Britt see in a man like that? Detectives aimed to find out the next day when they drove over the bridge from the Florida mainland to the world of those privileged enough to live in Palm Beach Shores.

When they arrived at the Britt's Claremont Lane home, detectives found Wanda to be welcoming and cordial, but if they expected to get an earful about a clandestine affair between boss and secretary, they were disappointed. Wanda said that she too had been the recipient of Dick's strange and awkward sexual advances, but that she had rebuffed them for the entire two years of her employment. Yes, she said, his modus operandi was the same as that he would use later with Glenda—ask her to stay late, after all of the other employees had gone home, invite her into his office and then lock the door. Instead of looking at her legs though, he wanted her to talk about her most intimate feelings, Wanda said.

"He would ask her all about her sex life and make some advances and then chicken out," according to detectives. "He would then apologize to her for his actions and it would appear to her that he was very insecure and wanted to prove himself."

Though Wanda had attended the Robison family funeral in Michigan the previous June, she told the detectives that she hadn't seen her boss for at least a year before he was murdered. When the crime had been discovered, she was in Florida with her husband, recuperating from complications after surgery and a miscarriage. Her husband did not know that she had worked for Dick Robison, she said, until the murders were reported in the news and she told him that the father of the murdered family was her former boss.

If the paternity of the baby Wanda lost to a miscarriage about the same time as the murderer was taking aim at the Robison family was a topic of discussion that day, it wasn't put in the detective's report. And neither was the odd coincidence of the positioning of the dresses worn by two of the women in Dick's life. At Dick's urging, Glenda Sutherland had hiked her dress up around her waist, thinking, at the time, who knows what. When her body was found, Shirley Robison was lying on her stomach, her dress pushed up around her waist as well, and certainly against her will, her thoughts more unknowable even than Glenda's.

The Robison family. Front, left to right: Shirley, Susie, Dick. Middle: Randy. Back, left to right: Gary, Ritchie.

Drive entering Blisswood from M-119. The route continues on past Chauncey and May Bliss's house and down a steep, vine-covered hill to the site of Summerset, the Robison cottage.

Summerset, the Robison cottage, hours after
the bodies were discovered

Officers gather outside the Robisons' cottage. Emmet
County prosecutor Richard Smith sits at the base of
the tree; Undersheriff Clifford Fosmore and an unknown
deputy stand nearby.

Emmet County undersheriff Clifford Fosmore, wearing a
gas mask, shows prosecutor Richard Smith the bloody hammer
found inside the cottage.

Law enforcement officers, wearing gas masks, investigating the murder scene

Left to right: Monnie Bliss, the Good Hart native who discovered the bodies, unknown man, Undersheriff Clifford Fosmore, and prosecutor Richard Smith

Undersheriff Clifford Fosmore inspects the bullet holes in an outside window of the Robison cottage.

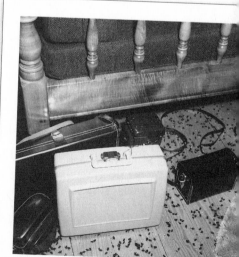

Handmade lock mechanism designed by Chauncey and Monnie Bliss

The Robisons' valuable camera equipment found inside the cottage and surrounded by dead flies

Superior Table

Mr. Roebert
Sylvia***

Mr. Richard
Joyce - Joe

Mr. Peters
Pam

Mr. Joseph
Betty

Mr. Martin
Gail

Mr. Thomas
staff

The above shows the chain of power as decided by Mr. Roebert, Chairman and Director of the Superior Table...the govern power of this world wide organization which is souly set on complete peace and unity among all countries of this Earth.

Each of the above mentioned directors will receive a complete organizational break-down from Computer Headquarters.

If you have any questions, please direct them through the proper channels.

Thank you,
Sylvia-Secretary to Mr. Roebert ***

cc; Mr. Richard ✓
Mr. Joseph
Mr. Martin
Mr. Thomas
Mr. Peters

Curious memo found among Dick Robison's papers

An Invitation

It is with great pleasure that we

offer you the

opportunity of becoming a

Member in the

Impresario Cultural Society

and participate in its many

advantages

centered around

world cultural activities

in and for all the arts

For Membership Information Write
IMPRESARIO CULTURAL SOCIETY
Lathrup Village, Michigan 48075

An invitation to join the Impresario Cultural Society, founded by Dick Robison

.25-caliber Beretta handgun, similar to what is believed
to be one of the murder weapons. The actual murder weapons
were never found.

Bloody shoe print left at the crime scene, presumably
by the killer

Joseph "Joe" Raymond Scolaro III, the Michigan State Police's chief suspect

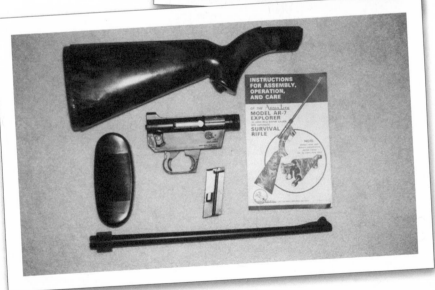

A disassembled AR-7 survival rifle, manufactured by Armalite. According to the company brochure, it could be reassembled in forty-five seconds.

Detective Lloyd Stearns talking with Joe Scolaro outside
Michigan State Police post

Joseph "Joe" Raymond Scolaro III

Michigan State Police detective John Flis searching for "brass" at a makeshift target range in Union Lake, Michigan, owned by Joe Scolaro's father-in-law

Inside Summerset, days before the cottage was torn down. The outline of Shirley Robison's body can still be seen.

```
The Alibi
```

```
                                    1968
```

```
The police told me I did it. And they
said if I didn't pull the trigger, I
know who did.
```

—Joseph R. Scolaro III, quoted in the *Detroit Free Press,*
November 8, 1970

State police detectives got a weird vibe off Joe Scolaro almost from the very moment they met him, and his presence in their interview room frustrated the detectives right from the start. First, he followed up his overtly friendly handshake with cagey answers to even their most basic questions. He showed an initial bravado about being Robison's "right-hand man," trusted to oversee all the day-to-day operations of the firm and to consult with Dick over the telephone when he was away on business. Just recently, Joe said, Dick had gone to San Francisco, and Joe ran everything while he was away. But as they dug deeper, asking about his boss's business trips and the firm's nitty-gritty financial details, his mastery changed into complete ignorance.

According to the state police report, their exchanges went like this:

Detective Lloyd Stearns: What would be the title you would have there?
Joe: Well, Dick told people I was his Executive Vice President . . . and that's what I was, I was his assistant. He explained it this way. When somebody would say, "You know, gee, what is Joe?" "Well he's my right arm."
Stearns: Ok, and what was your salary when you started work for Dick?
Joe: Oh, boy, that's a hard question because I don't even remember.
Stearns: Was [Dick] in the office most of the time?
Joe: Oh, he came in two days a week, something like that. . . . He operated out of his house.

Stearns: When did you first know about him going to San Francisco?

Joe: About three days prior he told me he was going out of town.

Stearns: Did you know what the nature of this trip was?

Joe: He just told me business.

Stearns: What do you mean? He apparently had some idea what type of business, whether it was to do with his magazine or
. . .

Joe: He said, "business" and I said, "Is this monkey business or business?" And he said, "No, its something to do with the magazine." And, that was it.

Stearns: About how many times did you figure he called you [from San Francisco]?

Joe: I couldn't really pin that down.

Stearns: At any time after he came back from that trip, did he tell you what the purpose of it was? Or the nature of the trip?

Joe: Well, he just told me that it was, when he came back, that it had to do with his master plan, all of the things he was involved with. . . . Dick was planning some fantastic growth, Lloyd. I don't know if you looked into it, but, I mean, it was really fantastic, enough to choke a horse!

Stearns: Where would I check on this at?

Joe: Well, uh, possibly different people would have told you, you know.

Stearns: Would it be on paper or anything?

Scolaro: Oh, I don't know if it would be on paper.

How could Joe have been given managerial free rein over both an active advertising agency and a bimonthly magazine, so that Dick could spend the summer up north, and still not know what the trip to the West Coast was about or what the plans to dramatically expand the business were, or even how that expansion was going to be financed? The detectives were skeptical, to say the least.

Further questioning by detectives revealed that this planned expansion, "fantastic . . . enough to choke a horse," included private airport hangars and personal pilots for executives, a centralized purchasing scheme with big warehouses of raw materials to supply area manufacturing companies, a cultural society, a performing arts news service, and television specials all based on the arts magazine Robison published, as well as commercial travel, student scholarships, and residential developments. For his part, Joe started throwing around large sums of money to detectives, saying $50 million or $100 million would be needed to fund such an enterprise, but insisted that he didn't know who any of Dick's business partners were, nor where the money was coming from. Detectives weren't sure if the plans were real and Joe was stonewalling them, or if they were just a strange and narcissistic fantasy of Dick's. Walter Muellenhagen had the same doubts.

On top of learning what the scheme was, how much it was going to cost, and where the money was coming from, now detectives had to figure out if the money was even real. They were certain Joe knew more than he was saying.

"You had a lot of contacts with this man, more than anybody else had," Detective Stearns told Joe. "He confides in you, there is no reason for you not to know detail. No reason in the world for you not to know."

"I'll try to fill you in on everything I can," Joe told them. They couldn't be sure if he was trying to be helpful, or just trying to look like he was.

The young executive told the detectives he found out about the murders while listening to WJR, a Detroit radio station. A round of phone calls ensued, and he, Shirley Robison's brother, and another business colleague chartered a plane from Detroit to Harbor Springs, where they were met by police and driven north. Despite his haste in making an appearance at the Emmet County sheriff's office just twenty-four hours after the bodies were discovered, something about the man continued to feel odd.

By now, police had already interviewed dozens of people, including family friends, neighbors, and relatives of the slain, and all had shared the same basic story. The Robisons didn't smoke or drink. They were active in their church. Their children were model youngsters. They didn't own handguns, as far as their neighbors knew—as a matter of fact, Dick didn't even hunt. It was a bit unusual, in fact, for a man who spent so much time up north. In short, the family had no history of gun ownership and no known enemies. Sure, Dick Robison could be dogmatic, even patronizing at times, but he had done nothing to provoke the frenzy of viciousness that had exploded inside the cottage's solid log walls. Nothing.

But then police talked to Joe. Although he would say nothing specific about the company's finances, he revealed other, more titillating details that police found immediately suspicious. Without much prompting, he told them about Dick's mysterious business trips, his own large expense account and recent bonuses, the blank but signed company checks he had possession of, the obsessive number of phone calls between himself and Dick just before the murders, and even his own alibi. Police hadn't even asked Joe to provide an alibi, but there it was. He said he had been at a plumbing convention at Cobo Hall in Detroit on June 25, the day police now believed the murders had taken place. And then there was that pair of .25-caliber Beretta pistols. One for Joe, one for Dick.

Guns? Alibis? Big money? The officers must have wondered what the churchgoing father had turned into. Something had happened to the respected businessman and loving husband they had been hearing so much about, almost to the point of disbelief. Something beyond shenanigans with his secretaries. This was a side of Dick that no one else had yet shared. A side that could be a lot closer to murder, despite the fact that they still didn't have a motive.

By the end of that first interview, police had Joe firmly pinned under their mental microscope of suspicion, and were about to turn him this way and that, adjust the focus to close up, and scrutinize this cagy specimen with every investigative technique at their disposal. They would dissect all aspects of the crime, and Joe's background was exactly where they planned to start poking around.

"He always came up with quick answers to questions; however, some of them did not appear logical and were not satisfactory to these officers," Stearns wrote in his report of that initial formal interview, dated August 7, 1968.

Even though they still didn't have a clear motive for the crime, detectives now at least had Joe's alibi.

* * *

On June 25, 1968, in the city of Detroit, it was raining. Hard. A flash summer downpour that swamped street sewers, collapsed umbrellas, slowed traffic, and flooded basements—including, Joe said, the basement under the well-tended white brick home at 18790 Dolores Street in Lathrup Village, the suburb of Detroit where the Robisons lived. The house was under Joe's care while the Robisons were up north in Good Hart, and so he said that he got up early that day, drove across town to check on the house, and found water dripping through a window well and into the basement.

Joe called Dick. "I'm here at the house. It's raining like crazy and I just wanted to let you know that there was water in the basement but I cleaned it right up," Joe said when he reached Dick by phone up at the cottage. "And don't worry about anything, everything down here is being taken care of."

According to Joe, Dick thanked him for cleaning up the mess, and then asked Joe if he had received the package of signed company checks he'd mailed to the office from the Good Hart General Store a week ago. Since April, Joe had been in charge of the day-to-day operation of the business, but even three hundred miles north, Dick still wanted to have the final say about finances and besides Shirley, he was the only signer on the company's checking account. Joe said he hadn't received anything, so Dick told him that he would call the bank and stop payment on the checks, just in case they'd been stolen or lost in the mail.

From Dolores Street, Joe told officers, he went to the post office to pick up the mail for R. C. Robison and Associates and found the missing checks in the day's bundle of letters. He drove to the firm's offices at 28081 Southfield Road in Southfield and called Dick back to let him know that the checks were safe.

"Okay," Dick said, "I'll let the bank know and tell them to remove the stop payment. I'm still planning to be up here for the rest of the summer, so if anyone's looking for me, tell them I won't be back in the office until the first of September. You can handle everything until then, right?"

Joe said that he could. "Good," Dick told him, "because we're leaving today on that trip south I told you about. First Kentucky, then Florida, and we won't be back to the cottage for a couple weeks, maybe longer. Don't expect us until at least the fifteenth or twentieth. I'll call you when we get back."

It was to be a real estate buying trip, Joe told the detectives. Dick would be looking at horse farms in Kentucky and oceanfront condos in Florida. The horse farm was to be a family retreat, especially for Susie, who, like most girls her age, was giddy for horses. The Florida condo was to be a surprise gift for his aging father, Ross.

"Are you flying?" Joe asked Dick.

"That hasn't been established yet. We may drive."

"Are you going with anyone?"

"That hasn't been completely established yet, either. If I go with somebody, you don't know who they are . . . so don't worry about it, pal."

That's where Joe's alibi begins to fall apart. He stayed in his office until about noon, he claimed, then drove to a Montgomery Ward store on 12 Mile and Telegraph to shop for a radio. He browsed for thirty or forty minutes in the store's electronics department and then left for the plumbing convention. Dick wanted him to go to the convention, Joe said, and check in with some of the company's biggest clients, Delta Faucet and Peerless, and a few new prospects like the Nile Corporation. He walked around the convention floor and stopped off at a few of the booths. He talked with a man named Norm Abbot, who had just been made sales manager of Nile, and another associate from Peerless named Bob Laidlaw. Laidlaw told Joe he was leaving the convention early because he had a date that evening.

Joe then went across the street to the Pontchartrain Hotel, where he had a couple scotch and sodas at the Salamander Bar. Then, he said, he decided to go shopping again—"I like to shop. It's relaxing."—and took a cab to Hudson's Department Store. He didn't meet anyone at the bar and didn't remember the bartender. He didn't buy anything or talk to anyone at Hudson's. He didn't get a receipt for the cab ride and he didn't get a parking ticket.

The rainstorm continued throughout the day, darkening the sky and soaking Joe through his raincoat and his suit jacket and down to the skin by the time he made it back to his car. It was raining so hard, in fact, that he told the detectives that there was water in the trunk of his car and even inside the taillights.

From where he parked on Telegraph, Joe said, he drove to the office to check if the roof there had leaked in the rainstorm. The office had a flat roof, and the downspout that drained it was notorious for getting plugged up with sticks and leaves and other debris. Just as he thought, it was clogged. Joe braved the pelting rain and cleaned out the pipe and called his wife from the office to let her know why he was so late getting home.

Then, Joe said, he decided to check the Robisons' basement one more time before he went home, and so he drove back to Dolores Street. By now it was almost dark. Just a little bit of water had leaked in since he last checked the house. He cleaned that up and then called the Robisons' neighbor, Margaret Smith, and talked with her for a while. After they finished their conversation, he tried to reach Dick up at the cottage, let the phone ring and ring, but hung up when there was no answer. Joe then headed for his house in Birmingham, telling the detectives the trip took longer than usual because of the downpour.

"I had my car and I winged my way home. Which was a hell of a job because I couldn't use Southfield. I ended up using Evergreen to get home and, you know, a lot of cars were jammed and it took me a hell of a long time to get home. But I got home."

By now, according to Joe, it was sometime between 11:00 p.m. and midnight, maybe even later. His wife, Lora Lee, and his son, little Joey, were sound asleep.

* * *

There were big problems with this itinerary. *Discrepancies* was the detectives' euphemism for what they could have just called lies. For starters, the plumber's convention at Cobo Hall was a three-day event, ending on June 25, the day that Joe said he attended and visited with clients. Joe said he left his office at noon, went shopping for a radio, and then went to the convention. If that were the case, he wouldn't have seen many clients, because by noon that day, according to a number of the attendees detectives interviewed, most exhibitors were breaking down their displays, packing them up to ship home, and getting ready to leave. By one o'clock, about the time Joe says he arrived at the convention, most of the booth spaces were already empty.

Detectives tracked down Bob Laidlaw, the Peerless executive Joe said he'd talked with. Laidlaw told detectives that yes, he had seen Joe at the convention, that they'd gone to a hospitality room at the Ponchartrain Hotel together, had a couple drinks, then walked back over to the convention. "He cannot say which day it was, but does recall that the weather was real nice and the sun was bright," Detectives Stearns and Flis wrote in their interview report.

The detectives also visited three local manufacturer's representatives from the Delta Faucet Company who attended the convention. Each placed Joe at the convention on June 24, not June 25.

Detectives inspected the basement of the Robison home, and found no water damage. They sent a police photographer to Dolores Street to document their findings.

The neighbor, Margaret Smith, didn't recall hearing from Joe on June 25, the night of the storm, and neither did Joe's wife, Lora Lee, though she did tell detectives that wet clothes and a wet overcoat were waiting for her in the laundry room when she woke up the next morning.

* * *

When they had shot as many holes in Joe's alibi as they could, Stearns and Flis again trained their sights on his guns. Though the second .25-caliber Beretta pistol, the one that Joe said he bought for Dick, had still not been found, detectives continued to believe it was one of the murder weapons. No other handgun tested at the state police crime lab on Harrison Road in East Lansing had even come close to exhibiting the characteristics of the murder weapon except Joe's. Officers were now almost certain that Dick and his family had been initially attacked with a .22 rifle, and then the killer used Dick's own gun to deliver the coup de grâce. The idea that two guns meant two killers was not absolute, especially where their chief suspect was concerned.

From their research into his background, detectives already knew that Joe served three years in the army. During his military service it was a "straight key," used for sending and receiving Morse code, and not a gun that was his primary assigned weapon, but Joe still knew how to shoot. He may have harbored an interest in firearms before he enlisted, or maybe he developed it while serving in the Army Security Agency, but whatever the source, the man loved his guns.

Joe competed regularly in state trap-shooting meets sponsored by the Amateur Trapshooting Association, traveling to target ranges around Michigan to test his skills against other shooters. The sport of trap shooting substitutes a clay disk, called a pigeon, shot into the air out of a trap machine, for the live birds that were released from wire cages or traps in the 1800s when the sport got its start. Shooters use a 12-gauge single- or double-barrel shotgun, aiming from five different positions at targets approximately twenty yards away. According to trap shooter Bill O'Connor, vice president of Capital City Rifle Club in Lansing, Michigan, in order to excel at the sport, participants must have shoulder strength, a clear focus, and good hand-eye coordination.

"You're shooting at a moving target that is traveling away from you at different angles," O'Connor says. "Sometimes you might hit it and a little chip breaks off, but sometimes you just smoke it. And that's where the satisfaction comes in. When nothing's left of the target but a little puff of smoke."

It was at a trap-shooting meet that Joe met a gun dealer by the name of Bill Herrington. Herrington lived in a house trailer on the property of one of the gun ranges Joe frequented. The two men became friends, and in early 1968 Joe told Herrington that he wanted to buy two pistols, one for his boss and one for himself.

The previous summer, Detroit erupted into a violent and deadly riot after police officers from the vice squad raided an illegal after-hours club. The confrontation escalated into a five-day riot, eleven square miles of the city were in chaos, and President Lyndon Johnson called in both the army and the National Guard to restore order. In the resulting melee, forty-three people were killed, more than seven thousand were arrested, another five thousand were left homeless, and close to two thousand buildings were burned.

Not surprisingly, in the months after the riot, gun sales soared, especially in the suburbs surrounding the city. Doctors, teachers, homemakers, autoworkers, businessmen—it seemed like everyone was buying a handgun. Even Dick Robison's close friend and neighbor, the peacefully minded Dr. Roger Smith, bought a pistol to use for protection when commuting to Detroit's Henry Ford hospital.

Dick told Joe that he, too, was on edge over the increased tension in the city, and despite the antigun editorial he had just published in his arts magazine, he wanted to buy a handgun. Joe talked to Herrington, and in February 1968 Herrington placed an order with the Williams Gun Sight Company in Davidson, Michigan, for two .25-caliber Beretta six-shot automatics and four boxes (one hundred rounds) of the Sako ammunition.

Herrington told police that Joe picked up the guns in April. Joe's wife, Lora Lee, confirmed the date, and said she was with her husband at the Birmingham Gun Club when he bought them. Once they got home, Scolaro put one of the guns in her purse drawer and the other in his dresser drawer, along with all of the ammunition. Though Scolaro told the detectives he had given the gun to Dick Robison in February or March, Lora Lee said the gun remained in her purse drawer until mid-June, when her husband took it with him to work. Later he told her he had given it to Dick.

In March 1969 detectives were surprised to learn that Joe bought a .22-caliber rifle at the Montgomery Ward store in Detroit at 12 Mile and Telegraph—the same store where he shopped for a radio on June 25, the day of the murders, according to his story. The date of the purchase was July 1, 1968, after the murders, but before the bodies were discovered. Was he replacing the .22 he disposed of after the murders with this new gun, officers wondered? Was he trying to keep the purchase under wraps by going to a department store instead of to a friend? The gun was a Glenfield model 60 semi-automatic made by Marlin. "It seemed unusual to officers that he would purchase the gun from Wards when he has numerous contacts with the Williams Gun Sight Co. and received discounts on trade name guns," Stearns and Flis wrote in their report. "All of his other guns are trade name guns and most of them are rather expensive."

By now, the state police had called in forensic accountants from the private sector and from the Oakland County prosecutor's office, and while these men followed the money, Stearns and Flis continued to follow the guns. On November 11, 1969, the two trails came together, and detectives got closer to the second murder weapon. The forensic accounting work found that in the months after his boss's murder, Joe's creative money management veered from desperation to outright fraud, and he was arrested for obtaining money under false pretenses. When they had him in custody, Joe assumed that he was being arrested for the murders and detectives questioned him again about the crime. Inexplicably, he told detectives that at one time he had owned two AR-7 Armalite .22-caliber semiautomatic rifles that he bought from his brother-in-law. Detectives had heard anecdotal evidence from Joe's neighbor, Karl Olbrich, that he had owned such a weapon, but the information had just been one more clue in an increasingly complicated case. Now they had Joe admitting freely that he owned not just one but two of the rifles. Not surprisingly however, he could produce neither for police to examine.

Joe said he gave one of the rifles to a friend, and fellow advertising executive, by the name of Hal Smirthwaite. The other rifle he gave back to Johnson.

* * *

The AR-7 is an interesting weapon with a tarnished reputation. It is the consumer version of an air force survival gun designed for use by pilots in the event they were either shot down or crash-landed and have to survive in the wilderness. It is lightweight—just two and a half pounds—and easily stored in a backpack; when disassembled, it is just sixteen and a half inches long. The AR-7 is also accurate up to distances of one hundred yards and the weapon's sight is adjustable for elevation and wind speed. Once fired, the shell casing is automatically ejected and the spring inserts another cartridge from its eight-round magazine. Drop the gun in a lake and it will float. According to the *Blue Book of Gun Values,* the main criticism of the AR-7 is its propensity to jam. However, anecdotal information collected on an AR-7 Internet forum states proudly that jammed guns don't make a loud sound when fired, allowing for a follow-up attempt before game can escape.

"Long rifle accuracy, hand gun convenience," the company stated proudly in its marketing materials. "No permits, none of the red tape regularly encountered through purchase and transportation of hand guns. The AR-7 Explorer can be stored in duffel bag, bed roll, larger tackle boxes, even carried in field jacket or mackinaw pocket." The whole gun could be disassembled or reassembled, the company said, in about forty-five seconds.

Curiously, in 1983 Armalite Inc. was purchased by the Marcos Philippine government, who moved the manufacturing operation from California to Manila two years later. Between its American and foreign owners, the company manufactured about 65,000 weapons. When Joe Scolaro bought his, 18,314 had been manufactured. Though it was not designed to be used with a scope, two companies—one in Plymouth, Michigan, J. B. Holden Company—manufactured retrofitted scopes that could be used with the AR-7.

The AR-7's dubious reputation, however, was made almost two decades after a rifle of this type was used on the Robison family. In 1983, Paladin Press, an independent publisher in Boulder, Colorado, released the now infamous book, *Hit Man: A Technical Manual for Independent Contractors*. Written under the pseudonym Rex Feral, the book has been portrayed in the courts and in news accounts as a how-to manual for contract killers. In 1997 a U.S. appeals court ruled unanimously that the book was not protected by any free speech laws after a triple murderer admitted to using it to plan his crime. The murderer was convicted of killing a mother, her eight-year-old handicapped son, and her son's nurse in a murder-for-hire case in Maryland in 1993. The gun recommended by *Hit Man*? The AR-7.

Joe, of course, could have no way of knowing that nearly twenty years after he bought the pair of AR-7 rifles, the very same model would be recommended in a notorious how-to guide for murder. Still, if he had been planning the crime when he bought the weapon, he certainly picked the right gun.

By the time the detectives met Herbert Johnson, Joe's brother-in-law was out of the gun business. In the fall of 1969, Johnson worked on a commercial construction job in Pontiac. Detectives called him at home and then visited him at work. To his credit, Johnson had kept good records of his sales and special orders while he was a gun dealer and could tell them that yes, he had sold Joe two AR-7s, one on September 30, 1966, and one on November 28, 1966. Yes, he had also been to the target range with Joe, and yes, they had taken turns shooting one of the AR-7s.

Detectives tracked down the advertising colleague of Joe's, Hal Smirthwaite, who supposedly had possession of one of the AR-7s Joe bought in 1966. Smirthwaite was now living in Chicago. Detectives paid him a visit, took possession of the AR-7 that Joe had indeed given to him, and secured his permission to conduct a ballistics test on the gun. Three days later, the Michigan State Police crime lab in East Lansing came to a dual decision on the weapon, which they promptly communicated to the detectives. The Robisons had indeed been shot with an AR-7, and it was ammunition from an AR-7 that made the bullet holes in the cottage's window. Just not *this* AR-7.

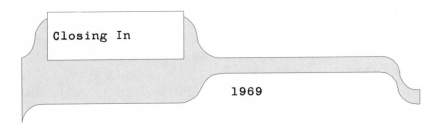

Closing In

1969

A week before Thanksgiving 1969, the state police finally sighted down on Joe Scolaro at, of all places, a Union Lake makeshift target range. It was there in the calf-high drying grass that their evidential condemnation of Dick's "right-hand man" went from just circumstantial to physical.

Police hadn't found Joe's Armalite AR-7 survival weapon, the one that was thought to be the rifle the killer used to pick off the first of the Robison family to die. What they did find, though, were spent shell casings fired from that very gun in two distinct places: The crime scene and now an amateur target range set up on property owned by Joe's father-in-law.

Joe had told police months ago that he gave the guns away, one to a friend in Chicago and one to the same man who had sold it to him in the first place, his brother-in-law, Herbert Johnson. Herbert was married to Lora Lee's sister, Judy. The Chicago AR-7 was tracked down and recovered, but the AR-7 that Joe supposedly gave to Johnson was never found, and police still believed this gun was one of the two murder weapons.

Herbert Johnson was not only Joe's brother-in-law, he was also a gun dealer, operating a little shop in Pontiac called The 5-V. If they're following the letter of the law, gun dealers keep detailed records on their sales, and Johnson could document the date of sale for all of his transactions with Joe, showing officers his copies of bill-of-sale receipts. He flatly denied ever receiving one of the guns back from Joe; if Joe *had* given him back the gun, he told police, there would have been something about it in his files, and there wasn't. Johnson said that Joe might have told him he wanted to return one of the guns, but never had.

"I didn't write up any records out of a clear blue sky," he said.

"Did he ever mention anything about the other gun coming back to you?" Stearns asked.

"Yeah."

"When would this be?"

"The other day, when he found out that I'd been talking to you."

"What'd he say about that?"

"He told me, he said, 'I told those people that you got the gun back. Don't you remember? I traded it back for some components.' And I didn't answer him because I didn't want to get involved in any kind of a conversation with him . . . I just didn't think it was the right thing to do to start B-S-ing with him about it."

Johnson showed police the firearms record book he kept up to date. He pointed out his "double-check" system; a number of entries were logged in, showing guns he bought from distributors or other gun dealers or individual customers and the guns he sold. Each entry had the customer's name, the serial number of the gun, and whether he had taken anything in trade. The AR-7 had a "clever" design, Johnson said, that appealed to Joe.

"He's an impulse buyer if there ever was one," Johnson said. "I mean, I know this for a fact. He can be walking by a store and see something in the window, and buy it just like that. If he had $50 in his pocket, he'd spend the $50 and hope that you thought he had another $500."

Johnson did offer up that a month or so after he'd sold him the guns, he and Joe had gone target shooting with one of the rifles sometime in 1967. They drove over to their father-in-law Albert Faulman's place on Elizabeth Lake Road. Faulman owned six acres of open fields there, with nothing to obstruct a bullet's path but an old Quonset hut, and a couple cords of seasoned firewood, making it a safe place to try out the AR-7. Johnson and Joe wanted to see how the novelty weapon would fire. Just how accurate it really was. They shot fifty shells through it, Johnson said. It fired pretty good.

"Do you think the brass might still be there?" Detective Stearns asked.

"Oh, it would definitely be there but it'd probably be a job finding it."

"Would you be willing to show us this place where it's at?"

"Yes."

* * *

It was a combination of good detective work and luck that uncovered the first piece of physical evidence linking Joe to the murders. If Joe had decided to try out the AR-7 he would later give to his Chicago friend instead of the one thought to be the murder weapon, or if he never went target shooting at all, or if he had gone by himself or if Johnson had not given the location to police, no trace of the gun would probably have ever been found. But a year and a half after the murders, each of these details marked the trail for police, which is why, during a stretch of good weather on November 12 and 13, 1969, Stearns and Flis found themselves tramping over fallen oak leaves and a tight weave of dead field grass, looking for evidence.

From early in the morning until it was too dark to see, they marked off sections of the Faulman property with white twine wrapped around sticks pounded into the ground in large rectangles, and combed through each one with a metal detector. The men found twenty-one shell casings that appeared to have been fired from an AR-7. Stearns took out a black marking pen and wrote his initials, "L.S." on each one before delivering them, at 9:15 the next morning, to the crime lab in East Lansing.

Faulman, who had given the detectives permission for the search, recalled the day that his two sons-in-law had been by to fire the weapon. He had gotten a good look at it. It was an unusual gun, he told the officers, and he knew no other Armalite rifle had been fired there.

On November 17, the crime lab had made their determination: "In my opinion at least five of the shells were fired in the same weapon as the four .22-caliber shells from the crime scene," Detective Charles Meyers wrote in his report. "Fifteen other shells exhibit similar characteristics and could have been fired in the same weapon as the evidence shells from the crime scene. One shell is not identified."

Years later, on July 22, 1988, the *Petoskey News-Review* ran a twentieth-anniversary article on the crime, stating that .22-caliber casings found at the crime scene and .22-caliber casings found at the Union Lake firing range closely matched, "but individual markings differed." Charles Meyers, now retired from the Michigan State Police and living in Florida, received a clipping of the article in the mail from a friend. He was so incensed at the "misquote" that he wrote a letter expressing as much.

"I'm certain that you know and would remember that the crime scene casings were positively identified as having been fired in the same firearm as five of the specimens from Scolaro's range," Meyers wrote. "That aside, I'll close by wishing you well and hoping that 'God's Country' is still, at least partially, preserved."

Back in 1969 though, it had taken untold man-hours, a metal detector, the keen eyes of the crime lab staff, one brother-in-law willing to turn in another, and of course good luck, but police now had their first piece of physical evidence, albeit circumstantial, against Joe Scolaro. The same gun that had open fired on the Robison family through the window of their

Good Hart cottage had also taken target practice on the back forty at Joe Scolaro's father-in-law's place. Joe owned two guns of this unusual make and model, and now couldn't account for one of them. Two witnesses saw Joe shoot this unaccounted for gun at the family target range. The next logical steps, officers Stearns and Flis had to be thinking, were a warrant for Joe's arrest, an arraignment where he would be formally charged, a trial where he would be convicted, a sentencing hearing, and finally, the chance to type the words "Closed By Arrest" on the paperwork for Case No. 7471.

To that end, the detectives began working on a report to submit to Emmet County prosecutor Donald Noggle and state attorney general Frank Kelley.

* * *

Even before Stearns and Flis paid a visit to his personal target range, this had not been a good couple weeks for Joe. He had been continually dodging bankruptcy in increasingly creative ways ever since he bought Dick's business from the family's estate, and now Joe's dreams of wealth were officially being shot down.

In mid-October, Joe sold *Impresario* magazine, Dick's pride and joy, to a printing company. He had no choice. He couldn't pay the printing bills, and this way he at least would still have a job. The printing company, Swenk and Tuttle of Adrian, Michigan, agreed to keep him on as an ad salesman. He also had to sell Dick's Cessna Sky Hawk, and found a buyer in Harry Ford, who still worked for Delta Faucet. All the trappings of Dick's executive lifestyle, the lifestyle that he worked for fifteen years to build, had slipped from Joe's hands in just over a year.

This same week, Joe also took his second polygraph test, this time administered by the state's top examiner of the day, Richard North. The questions North asked centered on the crime, the guns, and whether Joe had been at the cottage on the day the shootings occurred. According to North, Joe's responses "indicated deception."

"Do you know for sure who used the AR-7 to shoot the Robisons?" state police polygraph examiner Richard North asked him.

"No," answered Joe.

"Before it happened did you know an AR-7 would be used to shoot the Robisons?"

"No."

"Do you know where that AR-7 is now?"

"No."

"Did you lie to the police about giving that AR-7 back to your brother-in-law?"

"No."

North's opinion was that Joe's biological responses to these questions again "indicated deception." Joe was still resolute in maintaining his innocence. North noted in his report: "Post-test interview . . . failed to gain any admission."

On October 20, the Internal Revenue Service seized Joe's business in lieu of $14,000 in back taxes. While Stearns and Flis were crawling around on their hands and knees looking for evidence in Joe's father-in-law's field, IRS agents were cataloging and preparing his assets to be sold at auction.

A new magazine called *Showdog* that he had been trying to get started fell through, taking $10,000 of an outside investor's money along with it. Joe couldn't make the payments on a Jeep that he was trying to buy from a friend, and so the vehicle was repossessed. He owed another friend $4,765 and had written him a promissory note for the money, payable on March 2, 1973. The same friend had an uncashed check in his wallet from Joe for $850. Walter Muellenhagen had loaned him money, and so had Cal Mackey. And these were just the debts police knew about. There were probably more.

Joe had moved his office and started another business he called Dimensional Research in Southfield's Harvard Plaza East, a strip mall. Years ago, Joe had been a promising scholar at a prestigious ivy-league university; now, he was working in a strip mall that had borrowed its famous name.

Any remaining staff inherited from Dick's businesses he had let go because he couldn't pay them, and so now his mother, Kathleen Scolaro—"Kitty"—was working for him as his receptionist and secretary. The only thing new about this company though was its name. Joe continued to operate much as he had before. "The history of the Dimensional Research Inc. is that it was a company set up to conduct a check kiting scheme between the Security Bank and Trust and the Manufacturer's National Bank of Detroit," said the state police report.

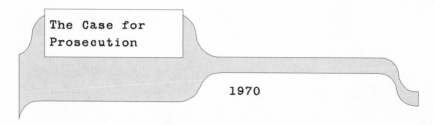

Robison murders believed solved

— Headline in the *Detroit News,* January 6, 1970

For the week leading up to the 1969 Christmas holiday, and for the following week before the New Year, and then for another week into 1970, a two-inch thick report detailing the entire police investigation to date sat untouched in the Emmet County Prosecutor's Office.

The report was the result of eighteen months of meticulous police work by detectives who had investigated the Robison case, gathered all the pertinent details, and then forged them into a single narrative. Here together for the first time was all of the background research, all of the interviews, the polygraph test results, the lab and autopsy results, and of course those crucial ballistics determinations.

The three-hundred-page report was physically heavy, but also loaded down with human expectations. So precious was their package that to Detectives Stearns and Flis, who drove north in order to hand-deliver their report safely into the care of prosecutor Donald G. Noggle, it must have felt like they were handing over pages plated with 14-karat gold.

For the past year and a half the men had been given free rein to work the case, their other responsibilities, for the time being at least, officially lifted and passed on to other detectives. Though the detectives didn't come right out and state it publicly, after devoting thousands of man-hours and experiencing incalculable mental strain and continuous public pressure to solve the case, the issuance of a warrant for the arrest of their chief suspect would have been a fitting return on their investment.

Their boss, state police director Colonel Frederick Davids, had already read the report, contributed to it even, but stopped short of officially requesting that Noggle issue an arrest warrant. He was willing to say, though, that such an outcome was a much-desired possibility.

"There is enough information in there for someone to act and we expect the prosecutor or the attorney general's office to respond that it contains enough to proceed to trial or not," Davids said.

In their summary, the lawmen detailed the murder weapons, the time of the crime, the discovery of the bodies, their chief suspect and his motive, which they had determined to be embezzlement. The report included this summary:

> The suspect was left in charge of the business for about three months prior to the murder and was left with signed blank checks. During this period his salary increased from $600 take home semi-monthly to $2000 take home semi-monthly. He was also receiving expense checks ranging from $300 to $1000 as often as twice a week. The investigation indicates that the victim was not aware of this until 6–25–68. This can be verified by the accountant and the records. It is believed that he did learn of it on 6–25–68 and confronted the suspect with it by phone 4 times.
>
> On 2–4–68 the suspect purchased two .25 caliber Beretta model 950-B pistols, serial numbers 47910 and 47836 along with 100 rounds of .25 caliber SAKO brand ammo. The suspect still has serial number 47910 which has been checked out. Serial number 47836 is missing and the suspect states he gave this gun along with the 100 rounds of SAKO ammo to the victim on the day after he purchased them. However, officers' investigation has failed to turn up anything that would substantiate this. (NOTE: The suspect's wife told officers that the suspect had both of the guns at the house from the time he purchased them until about June, 1968 when he took one of them to work one day. About a week later he told her that he had gave the gun to the victim.) The SAKO brand ammo is so rare that neither the laboratory officers or the field officers could locate any of it in Michigan for comparison. Some was eventually obtained from the Military Intelligence.
>
> On 9–30–66 the suspect purchased an ARMALITE, model AR-7, 22 caliber rifle, serial #68314. On 11–28–66 he purchased another like rifle with serial #75878. Shortly after he purchased #68314 he gave it to a friend in Chicago. Officers have checked this gun out and it was not the weapon used in the murder. Sometime in warm weather, believed to have been in the spring or summer of 1967, the suspect and his brother-in-law fired #75878 on some private property near Union Lake. Officers recently checked that location and located numerous empty casings. The crime lab has

checked these out and has identified these as having come from the same gun that was used in the murder. The suspect advised officers that he had given this gun to his brother-in-law sometime prior to the murders but this has been found to be false. This gun is also still missing. NOTE: This gun is so rare and unusual that even most sport and gun shops have never handled or even seen them.

On 6–25–68 the suspect left the office in Lathrup Village about 11:00 a.m. and didn't arrive home until after 11 p.m. This is by his own statement and was confirmed by his wife. He gave officers an alibi as to his activities and whereabouts on that day but officers have checked this out and found it to be false. Respectfully submitted, Det. Lloyd C. Stearns #85, Det. John Flis #2, Second District Headquarters.

Why it took Noggle more than three weeks to open the report and give it the benefit of his full attention is the subject of conjecture. He was either purposely antagonizing the police, overwhelmed by the scope of the case, tied up with his regular responsibilities, or maybe just methodical by nature. Perhaps each one of these hindrances and unknown others came into play between December 17 and January 13.

"I have been busy with other matters but will attempt today to start my search on the case," Noggle told *Petoskey News-Review* reporter Fred Lovelace on January 7. The prosecutor made a point to note to the newsman that the report was organized chronologically, without the benefit of cross-referencing or an index. These additions, he intimated, would have made the report more immediately accessible.

* * *

In January 1970, Noggle was sixty-seven years old, and at the tail end of a long and varied career in criminal justice. Freshly matriculated from Pontiac Junior College and the Detroit College of Law, in the early 1940s Noggle had been serving as chief assistant prosecutor for Oakland County when an unexpected event launched him into the county's top spot. That event was a possible suicide and the victim was his boss, Oakland County prosecutor Charles L. Wilson. The conjecture was that Wilson put a gun to his head and pulled the trigger rather than face a corruption investigation. Noggle was appointed to replace him and served as the county's top prosecutor from late in 1944 until 1946 in one of Michigan's most active courts.

In the fall of 1946, Noggle joined the legal staff of Brigadier General

Telford Taylor, chief prosecutor of twelve of the thirteen Nuremberg trials beginning in 1945 and ending in 1949. Here in a German courtroom, Noggle would have heard tales of mass atrocities that must have crossed his mind later when reviewing the crime scene photos in the Robison case. He also had the opportunity in his work with General Taylor to see a master trial attorney hammer the word of law into the minds of some of the most deadly men ever prosecuted.

Noggle and his wife, Gwendolyn, stayed in Europe for a few years after the end of the Nuremberg trials while he worked in various posts for the U.S. military courts, and then the couple moved to northern Michigan in 1955. Noggle worked first as a private practice attorney in Petoskey, then served as Emmet County prosecutor in 1957 and 1958, and again from 1969 to 1973. After working in a busy Oakland County court, then as part of General Telford's large staff, and finally with the full backing of the U.S. armed forces in the European-based military courts, being a lone wolf in Emmet County could have come as a bit of a shock.

In his county post, Noggle was now a one-man operation, prosecuting cases and providing legal counsel for the county's board of supervisors on whatever civic issues arose. Noggle had already said that, should the Robison case ever come to trial, he planned to defer to the state attorney general and let his staff prosecute.

"It would undoubtedly be a lengthy trial and as the only legal voice for the county, I feel I would be doing an injustice to the county as well as the case if I attempted to try it myself," Noggle told a reporter for the *Detroit News.*

Despite his workload and the holidays, detectives still may have expected to hear something official on their report before the middle of January. But Noggle stood mum on it until January 13, nearly a month after Stearns and Flis had personally delivered it to him. On that day he announced his determination on the value of its contents, and what he said could not have sat well with the state police: There was not enough evidence to issue a warrant.

The report detailed that Joe had failed three lie detector tests, could not account for at least eleven hours of his time on the day of the murders, had a financial motive to commit the crimes, knew the exact location of the Robisons' remote cottage, and had once owned guns the same make and model as both of the murder weapons.

What the report didn't do was place Joe at the scene of the crime at the time of the murders. Detectives had to be able to do that, or get an outright confession, before Noggle would issue an arrest warrant for the man.

Attorney general Frank Kelley had received a duplicate copy of the report from the state police, and after his review, he came to the same conclusion, standing firm with Noggle and fully supporting the county prosecutor's decision.

Back in November there had been a meeting on the case in Lansing with Colonel Davids, Detectives Stearns and Flis, nine other state police officers, Noggle, and Sheriff Zink. The men reviewed the case together, and Noggle had determined then that a warrant was premature. On January 13, after reading the report, Noggle said that it contained no new information and nothing in the investigation had changed. "At the conclusion of that conference [in November], Mr. R. C. Goussy, chief of the criminal division of the Attorney General's office, and I expressed our opinions that there was not sufficient evidence at that time to establish a prima facie case for criminal action," Noggle wrote in a January letter to Sheriff Zink, "and that further effort should be made to locate a murder weapon or weapons, or to place a suspect at the scene of the crime."

What Noggle may not have known, however, was that between the November 1969 meeting in Lansing and the day they turned in their report in Petoskey, Stearns and Flis had called on the wisdom of yet another legal mind. Ronald Covault, who was a chief assistant Oakland County prosecutor in Pontiac, was given the details of the case in early December. The murder had not happened in his county, and so his opinion would not be binding, but at least the detectives received the answer they were seeking. "[A]fter doing considerable research [Covault] advised that in his opinion there was sufficient information for issuance of a warrant."

Noggle, of course, believed otherwise and it was his opinion that mattered. In the Michigan court system the prosecutor presiding over the county in which a crime takes place is the person with the authority to issue an arrest warrant in the crime. The state attorney general can usurp the county prosecutor's decision, but in this case Kelley was backing Noggle all the way.

Though Noggle made an adamant public pledge to stick with the case until it was solved, and commended the detectives on their "hundreds of hours of tedious work thus far expended in this investigation," his words could not have offered much comfort to the two men who wanted an arrest warrant and nothing less. Stearns and Flis had no recourse now except to get back to work on solving the case, filling their days with the same inner grit and professional endurance they had brought to bear on their search for the killer or killers of the Robison family over the past year and a half. That is exactly what they did.

* * *

The next time the state police heard anything of substance from Noggle was in the spring of 1970, when the gist of a peculiar letter Noggle wrote to Capt. Daniel Myre made its rounds throughout the ranks. Noggle wanted detectives to take a closer look at the man who discovered the crime, Monnie Bliss.

Noggle's letter was quickly followed up by another, this in the form of an official "statement" from John "Bob" Clock, a reporter for the *Petoskey News-Review* who had been covering the case for his newspaper. Both letters suggested that police should be focusing their attention not on Joe Scolaro, but instead on a man much closer to the scene of the crime, Monnie Bliss. Noggle laid out eleven points that detectives should investigate, including a report of animosity between Monnie and Dick, a "cold" attitude on Monnie's part about his own son's death, and odd statements he made to police. Reportedly he had joked, "How much time am I going to get for this?" To Noggle, these were each suspicious and, taken together, even more so.

"[He] is a lifelong resident of the area," Noggle wrote "and . . . knows the cottage floor plan, area, paths, and roads well. It would be possible that Monnie Bliss may be a schizophrenic and would be a bad subject for the polygraph test and thereby produce the result heretofore determined. . . . Request that this communication be treated confidentially by your department and other law enforcement 'have to know' agencies."

His suspicions were supported by Clock.

"My impressions," Clock wrote in his statement, "are the result of frequent visits to the area and conversations with many of the residents. I believe, essentially, that the Robison case involved seven murders—not six—and that the Robisons were slain because they had knowledge of, or were suspected to have knowledge of, the first murder, that of Norman Bliss, 18."

Norman Bliss was the only son of Monnie and his wife, Dorothy, killed in a motorbike accident north of Good Hart on June 23. When it got to be four in the morning and their son still hadn't come home from a gathering with friends in the neighboring town of Cross Village, Monnie and Dorothy called the house where they thought Norman had gone and were told that he had left hours ago and said he was heading home. The drive from Cross Village to Blisswood is only seven miles, so Norman certainly should have been home in twenty minutes at the most, not three hours.

The couple decided to get in their car and drive toward Cross Village to see if they could find their son. Maybe his motorbike, a little Honda, had broken down, or run out of gas. Maybe he was too tired to drive and had stopped to sleep, or was hurt, alone somewhere in the night. They didn't have to drive far before they had the answer of what had happened to their son. Monnie and Dorothy found Norman lying on the ground a few feet off the road. His motorbike was nearby, also on the ground, at the base of a large tree. Norman's left leg was broken and though he had been wearing a helmet, his face was bloody. By the time his worried parents arrived at the scene, their only son was already dead.

Norman hadn't been murdered, according to the accident report and the county medical examiner. The official cause of death was skull fracture and cerebral hemorrhage caused when he missed a turn and his motorbike hit a tree.

A test by the Michigan Department of Health in Lansing would later show his blood alcohol to be .13. That would mean he had consumed three or four drinks. Current law in all fifty states uses .08 or above as the threshold for impairment and grounds for a citation.

In his statement, Clock theorized that Monnie had caused the accident by stringing a long wire cable across the road, murdering his son so that Norman would not inherit the Bliss family fortune. Monnie had tried to commit the crime earlier, on May 25, 1968, Clock stated, but a car driven by a Bliss family cousin hit the cable instead. He further theorized that one or more members of the Robison family had witnessed Monnie being up to no good, and that is why they were killed. Clock wrote that he was making his statement at the urging of Noggle, and requested immunity from any related libel laws. Clock also readily admitted that he had no hard facts to back up his theory, but instead relied on his acute knowledge of human nature honed over his years of news reporting experience.

As a newspaper reporter for the past 20 years, I am naturally hesitant to set down my impressions of the Richard C. Robison murder case. In my business, I deal chiefly with "facts" and "truth," insofar as they can be ascertained. In discussing the Robison murders, I have very few facts at my disposal and the truth about [what] actually happened to the Robison family certainly is not known by me.

However, I believe my role as a newspaperman may lend some weight to what I have to say. I make my living observing and interrogating and I firmly believe there are aspects of the Robison case which deserve a more thorough investigation than they have been afforded to date.

At the outset, let me say that I am making this statement at the request of Emmet County Prosecutor Donald Noggle. In order to protect myself and members of my family, I must insist that this document be made available only to those law enforcement people working on the Robison murders. I also must request immunity from the libel laws of Michigan on grounds that this statement does not constitute publication of my views and that I am without malice or prejudice in setting forth my opinions.

The first time I met Monnie Bliss was the day after the Robisons' bodies were discovered. I had been sent to Good Hart to attend a press conference called by law officers investigating the case. While crime lab detectives were working over the bodies inside the Robison cottage, I made it a point to introduce myself to Monnie Bliss. . . . [W]hen the Robisons' bodies were being removed from the cottage in their plastic bags, Monnie's fast, running commentary went something like this: "Death never bothered me one bit. Used to work for an undertaker in Harbor Springs and I didn't mind being around dead people. Some people get all upset about death. They hate to hit a squirrel on the road. But it doesn't bother me at all." Monnie did not appear to be the least bit affected by the grisly scene unfolding before us although he, among all those present, was the only one who actually knew the Robisons. As a reporter, I thought at the time that Monnie Bliss was someone the police should look at very carefully.

There was also an unsubstantiated rumor, Noggle and Clock both stated, that Monnie was missing a hammer.

* * *

So unattached to any part of the investigation were these missives from Noggle and Clock that the pages they were typed on must have seemed like they floated into state police headquarters from the clouds covering the Michigan sky, instead of arriving via first-class mail.

Monnie did not own a .25 Beretta or a .22 AR-7, the agreed-on murder weapons. He had already passed a lie detector test, and his hunting rifle was test-fired and cleared. Officers had interviewed every person in Good Hart who would talk, and although Dick Robison and Monnie Bliss were not friends and did not socialize, no one had mentioned an outright feud between them. Monnie was a compassionate man, his family said, and if he had any quarrel with Dick, it was because of the overly strict way Dick treated his children. The harshest words they could document from Monnie directed at Dick were from an interview with his carpenter's helper, Steve Shananaquet: "Monnie called him a 'crazy rich man,'" Steve said.

Clock lived in Charlevoix, and not Good Hart. Although Charlevoix is only forty miles to the south and the communities share the same daily newspaper, the same Little Traverse Bay, and the same county government, as far as knowing what was going on day to day in Good Hart, Clock might has well have been reporting from the moon. If he were from Good Hart, Clock would have known that Monnie was famous for his chatterbox style. His mind was so quick, his friends said, that his words nearly always came out in a jumble. The man talked a constant stream of announcements as if he were an omniscient narrator cataloging every action of his day, whether mundane or significant. What had seemed nefarious to Clock was endearing to Monnie's family and friends.

"He was a non-stop talker," says Bill Glass, a carpenter who worked with Monnie and has continued to build cottages in the area in the Bliss style. "He talked from the time he woke up, jabbered all day long. He never shut up. And he talked so fast that he'd get spit in the corner of his mouth . . . it was basically an endless tape of just reciting everything that ever happened to him."

To the detectives, Noggle's and Clock's view of Norman's accidental death as a premeditated murder must have seemed far-fetched and cruel.

Still the men had a duty to check out any and all tips in the ongoing investigation, and so yet a third meeting was called, this time in East Lansing, for the specific reason of discussing the contents of the two letters. Assignments were made for further investigation, but not to Stearns or Flis—they did not give the theory credence and were busy with Joe Scolaro. Detective Sergeant John Jurecic was to reinterview two of the first officers on the scene about Monnie's behavior, reinterview Steve Shananaquet about the missing hammer, reinterview Monnie himself, and obtain all the crime scene photos from the Emmet County Sheriff's Office and the *Petoskey News-Review*.

Detective Jurecic spent two weeks in April completing his tasks, and mostly came up empty. The rumor of the missing hammer was hatched over drinks at Leggs Inn, a bar and restaurant in Cross Village, lubricated no doubt by liquor.

When Jurecic interviewed Troopers Lawrence and Hancock they confirmed that Monnie had indeed made the odd statement "How much time am I going to get for this?" at the crime scene, but he said it in October, almost four months after the crime, and not the day they arrived on the scene. They had not questioned him further because they both agreed he was making a morbid joke—the kind compassionate but socially awkward people make in uncomfortable and tragic situations when they don't know what to say. Monnie walked up to their police cruiser, the troopers said, stuck his head in the open window and asked them the flip-sounding question, then chuckled. Inappropriate certainly, but no murder confession.

1970

I have the information and know the
killer of the Richard C. Robison
Family in Good Hart--Michigan in June
of 1968. . . . There is a time to talk
and now is the time Sir.

—Letter from a Leavenworth Federal Penitentiary
inmate to the Michigan State Police, January 12, 1970

Imaginary airport cultural centers, homegrown schizophrenics, missing murder weapons, and furtive locals. Each of these fruits of the crime and more had been been dealt with by state police detectives Lloyd Stearns and John Flis and now Patrick Lyons. By the beginning of 1970, the crime had gone unsolved for more than a year and a half. It is hard to imagine they were surprised when a letter from an inmate at a maximum-security federal prison a thousand miles away was added to the mix.

Through an unrelenting series of bad luck, bad choices, and bad deeds, Alexander Bloxom, a black man from Alabama born on Halloween Day in 1930, ended up in Leavenworth Federal Penitentiary by his fortieth birthday, wearing prison-issue duds and inmate number 85712. Years of weightlifting inside prison had well muscled him, and he was now a wire-wrapped brick of a man at five feet five and two hundred pounds. Small scars marked the center of his forehead, and his prisoner card described his eye color as "maroon."

Bloxom's path to Leavenworth was neither straight nor narrow. Instead, it wound through Kilby Prison in Birmingham, Alabama, for eight incidents of grand larceny in fifteen months; the U.S. Army's Sand Hill detention barracks at Fort Benning, Georgia, where the provost marshal there dishonorably discharged him for "undesirable character"; Jackson Prison in Jackson, Michigan, for murder, robbery, breaking and entering, and leaving the scene of an accident; Marquette Branch Prison in Michigan's Upper Peninsula for escaping from Jackson Prison; and finally, back down to Jackson in September 1957 for escaping from Marquette.

The State of Michigan had a hard time keeping its hands on Alexander Bloxom, but by April 1968, those in charge still had to parole him for time served, and so he was assigned to a parole officer and set loose in Detroit. Bloxom moved into a halfway house on Second Avenue, where he met all manner of ex-convicts and parolees, at least one of whom would be his future rap buddy.

By his own admission, Bloxom spent this first razor-blade-sized bit of freedom in more than two decades in the company of thugs more wanton even than him. The timing of his four months on the outside, and the letter he wrote and mailed from Leavenworth to the Michigan State Police, are what created an intersection between the lifeline of this black career criminal from the South, and the deaths of a white suburban family from the North. Part of his letter has been quoted at the beginning of this chapter. Here is more of what he wrote:

> I have the information and know the killer of the Richard C. Robison Family in Good Hart—Michigan in 1968. Also of four Robbery in Detroit and Belleview Michigan. I Can Not keep this inside of me any longer Knowing that I am in Prison For 25 years on a Bank Robbery that I had no Part of. There is a time to talk and now is the time Sir.

Bloxom's letter found its way into the hands of Daniel C. Myre of the Michigan State Police in East Lansing. A quick check found that Alexander Bloxom had been out on parole from April 3, 1968, until he was arrested for parole violation and bank robbery on July 25, 1968. Myre saw that in the previous twenty-one years the man had enjoyed not even four full months under an unbarred sky, and yet the timing of the Robison murders fell just about smack dab in the middle of those few precious free days. Though his motives for writing were questionable, Bloxom's letter interested Myre enough that the captain set to work on his own correspondence about the matter on the very next day.

"Because inmates often try to help themselves by furnishing the police false information, and in an attempt to determine if this is being done in the case of Bloxom, we respectfully request that Alexander Bloxom be interviewed," Myre wrote to special agent Jack H. Williams, care of the Topeka office of the Kansas FBI. Myre wasn't going to let a convict pull his chain, but he wasn't going to pass up a possible lead in an unsolved Michigan homicide, either. Professional courtesy was honored, and Special Agent Williams paid a visit to prisoner 85712.

By February, Myre had received Williams's official report of the FBI agent's interview with the prisoner. Yes, Bloxom was trying to get loose of a bank robbery conviction. Yes, he had been in prison since his teens. And yes, he was ratting out his rap buddies, but there was still something about Bloxom's far-fetched account of the Robison murders that could not be filed away in a drawer marked "False Confessions" and then forgotten. Not yet, anyway.

Michigan State Police detectives Lloyd Stearns and Patrick Lyons were headed for the plains of eastern Kansas.

* * *

By February 1970, Alexander Bloxom had fully experienced the "punishment, deterrence and incapacitation" that was the cornerstone of daily life for those unlucky, uncontrolled, or just plain bad enough to have ended up at Leavenworth. Inside "The Big Top," as the prison is nicknamed, in deference to the architecturally odd concrete dome crowning the massive facility, there was certainly no circus-type atmosphere to be found. And Bloxom wasn't going anywhere now unless he could talk his way out, despite his two short-lived but successful escapes from other prisons. Here, the rebar-and-concrete walls were not only forty feet high, but went down forty feet deep underground.

When his visitors from Michigan arrived, chaperoned by Agent Williams, Bloxom told them he did not need an attorney, he just needed to talk. Stearns, Lyons, and the FBI man sat across from Bloxom in one of Leavenworth's interview rooms and listened to him do nothing but that for two days. His story went something like this.

In Room 26 at the Detroit halfway house where he lived after being paroled, Bloxom became reacquainted with an old, skinny white man named Mark Warren Brock. Brock, whom Bloxom first met in Jackson Prison, was sixty-six years old and, like Bloxom, had been inside since his youth. The two became confidants, and though Bloxom was testing out the idea of going straight and had a steady job, he still began following whatever instructions, no matter how risky or wrongheaded, the older man gave him.

When Brock gave him money and an assignment to buy a car, Bloxom went to Motor City Dodge and picked out a 1963 black sedan. When Brock told him to come home from his orderly job at Grace Hospital so that he could drive Brock an hour north to Flint for an appointment, he drove him. When Brock told him to let him out at a Colonel Sanders and wait for him in the parking lot, he did it. When Brock came out of the fried chicken restaurant with a tall, bookish-looking stranger, and held a finger to his lips, Bloxom kept his mouth shut. On Friday, June 21, 1968, when Brock told him that he was headed up north on a job and that Bloxom couldn't come along because "there weren't no colored men up in Good Hart," he obliged him. And finally, when Brock told him to hand over the keys to the Dodge, right now, and don't forget the title and the registration, he did that, too.

"I saw that other man in the parking lot. I saw him real good," is what Bloxom told the officers. "He was white, fifty years or thereabouts. And big. Six foot, maybe two hundred, two twenty. He came up to our car, leaned his head in and said that if Mr. Brock does his job well, Joseph Scollata or Scolaro, something like that, will make sure that Mr. Brock is taken care of well."

Brock then got back in their car and the other man got into a 1967 or 1968 "robin's egg blue" Ford Thunderbird.

Brock went to Toledo to buy some guns before he went up north. Maybe he, Bloxom, went along, maybe not. The following Thursday, June 27, Brock returned to the halfway house with no explanation for his six-day absence and gave Bloxom back the keys to the Dodge. "Take it over to your people's house and put it up on jacks because I want it out of circulation." Again, Bloxom did as he was told.

"He came up to my room late, after supper but that day, and he brought in a briefcase. A smooth leather one. Brown leather. It had a zipper running all the way around and maybe some gold initials, I'm not sure. He opened it up and showed me a paper where he'd written out what I should do just in case he came up dead. I should read what was wrote, and do what it said."

Inside the briefcase, according to Bloxom, were investment bonds, eight or ten canceled checks with a rubber band around them and the words "Richard Robison Company" printed in the upper left-hand corner, three rolls of tape for a Dictaphone machine, and a photograph of a man, a woman, and four children standing on a boat. Brock took all these things out of the briefcase and put them in a manila envelope and taped up all four sides and hid it in Bloxom's closet. Then Brock pulled out a bread knife and cut up the briefcase and the two men went outside and burned the pieces of leather in the alley behind the halfway house.

By late July 1968, Bloxom was getting homesick for the South, and told Brock that he wanted to go visit his parents and his brothers and any other kin still alive in his native Alabama. Brock gave him not only his blessing but enough cash to buy a new Pontiac Bonneville for the trip, the manila envelope, a heavy black suitcase, and another assignment: get rid of the suitcase and get rid of it for good. Yes, it was heavy as hell, and no, he couldn't look inside because it was locked up tight and there wasn't going to be no key. Bloxom told the officers that he never did look inside; the only thing he could fathom that was that heavy, that size, and that hot were guns.

"I took my Aunt Mary and my cousin and we drove down to Birmingham in that Bonneville and stayed at my mother and daddy's place near the foundry," Bloxom said. "One day I went over to there, to the foundry, and I heaved that case into one a the rusted out boxcars bound for the furnace."

With his relatives now sufficiently visited and his disposal task complete, Bloxom needed to get back to Detroit if he was going to report to Brock, keep his job, and stay right with the parole board. Before he left Birmingham, though, he told his younger brother, Roosevelt Bloxom, about the secret envelope and showed him the spot in their parents' bedroom where he had hidden it. If anything happened to him, Bloxom said, echoing Brock's words of a month earlier, Roosevelt should open the envelope and follow the instructions inside. Bloxom returned to Detroit on July 23, but not before he heard his little brother say that he knew of a much better place to hide a secret than in a cubbyhole, underneath a pressboard chifforobe, on Twenty-eighth Avenue in Birmingham. Roosevelt was headed for Chicago and so was that envelope.

The day Bloxom arrived back in Detroit, he, Brock, and three other men were arrested for bank robbery and held over for trial at the Wayne County Jail. All five were found guilty of robbing the National Bank of Detroit at Fourteenth Street and Grand River. Bloxom was bound for Leavenworth, Brock for a federal prison in Atlanta, and the other three criminals for prisons unnamed. Before they parted ways, Bloxom says that Brock confessed to killing the Robison family—he and an accomplice named Robert Matthews did the now notorious deed.

The hearsay officers heard then went like this: "We went to the cottage and knocked on the door and I faked a heart attack," Bloxom said Brock told him through the bars of their jail cells. "While I was lying on the floor and Mr. Robison was trying to help me, Matthews came in and started shooting. The wife was the first one down and then one of the kids tried to run so we took him down too. Then, we just kilt 'em all."

While Bloxom said again he didn't rob any bank, he did tell officers that while he lived in the halfway house, he drove the getaway car while Brock and two other men robbed two gas stations, a drug store, and a liquor store. When Bloxom finished his story, the officers showed him some photographs. Do you see the man Brock met with in the Colonel Sanders? they asked him. Bloxom pointed to a photograph of Joe Scolaro. Then, considering his choice, he changed his mind and said he didn't think it was the same man.

"Go and talk to Brock if you want. Or hook me up to your machine," Bloxom challenged Lyons, Stearns, and Williams. "I'll take your liar's test."

Lyons and Stearns made arrangements to get a polygraph man to Leavenworth, then headed south to Atlanta.

* * *

With the help of the U.S. Marshal's Office in Atlanta, the detectives secured an interview with Mark Warren Brock on February 11, 1970, at the federal prison in Atlanta. "It should be noted at this time that this subject is sixty-seven years old and has spent forty-seven years of his life in prison," they stated in their report.

Yes, Brock knew Bloxom. Knew him well, in fact. Yes, he gave him money to buy a Dodge and a Bonneville. Yes, they cut up and burned a briefcase together, and yes, they did a few small-time robberies together too. Yes, he went to Toledo to buy guns. Yes, Brock knew his way around northern Michigan, and yes he took a trip up there in June 1968. Yes, he and Bloxom spent time at the same halfway house and yes, one time Bloxom did drive him from the halfway house to a fried chicken restaurant in Flint.

> Troopers: Did you have an appointment to meet with anyone inside that restaurant?
> Brock: I could have.
> Troopers: Did you keep that appointment?
> Brock: I could have met someone there on a business deal.
> Troopers: Have you ever been approached to be a trigger man?
> Brock: Yes, about three times.
> Troopers: When was the last time?
> Brock: June of '68.
> Troopers: Would you have ever considered taking on this kind of job?
> Brock: If the price was right, sure I would. Say, five grand at least.

Troopers: Mr. Brock, did you kill the Robison family?
Brock: No.

Brock told Lyons and Stearns that on each and every one of his many past criminal convictions, including this most recent one for bank robbery, he'd pleaded not guilty but been "fingered by a rap buddy." Despite such poor treatment by the men of his own circle, this type of selfish behavior still went against his own code of ethics. He had never fingered anyone, and he wasn't about to start now, even knowing as he did that with the current time levied against him, he was destined to die in prison. Brock then told the officers that he wasn't about to be subjected to a lie detector test, either, so don't even ask about something like that.

"I'm not going to tell you anything I might know about the murder of that family. If I ever change my mind, I'll let my parole officer know, but it ain't too likely you'll be hearing from me."

* * *

Police did not know quite what to make of the boulder of transgressions and truth that had solidified inside this man named Alexander Bloxom. Some of what he told them checked out. For example, his details about the robberies in Detroit of the drug store, the gas stations and the liquor store, including the dates, times, and items stolen, corresponded exactly to the police reports. His account of his time at the halfway house, his hookup with Mark Warren Brock, and, perhaps most inexplicably, his description of Richard Robison's brown leather briefcase, were dead accurate, too: Three secretaries, a janitor, and one of Robison's advertising colleagues separately confirmed that Robison had a briefcase exactly like the one Bloxom described. A potential investor in Robison's cultural centers plan, Ellis Jeffers, would tell the *Detroit Free Press* that during one meeting, Robison pulled a sheaf of drawings and notes about the centers out of a tan, cowhide briefcase.

"Strangely, police have never found the plans or the briefcase," the *Detroit Free Press* reported in an article published on November 8, 1970. "And [Joe] Scolaro said [he] didn't remember Robison having such a briefcase."

However, police were also convinced that Bloxom was lying when he said that he wasn't involved in the robbery of the National Bank of Detroit. Here was a prisoner in a maximum-security prison, looking at twenty-five years under the Big Top with no route to freedom but his mouth. He was almost thirty years younger than Brock, so time shaved off his sentence would mean something to him. Prisoners' stories about guilt and innocence, being in the wrong place at the wrong time, or just the hapless victim of another man's grudge needed nothing more than a mix of time and desperation to develop legs and run wild, and that, Lyons and Stearns would have surmised, could easily be the case here.

"It may be noted that officers feel there is little doubt but what Bloxom participated in the bank robbery after reviewing the case with the F.B.I. agents," the detectives wrote in their report of the interviews.

Still, they decided to check up on the two pieces of physical evidence that could tie Brock to the Robison murder—the black suitcase of guns and the manila envelope—and so they headed south again, this time to Alabama.

Upon their arrival in Birmingham, officers paid a visit to the U.S. Pipe and Steel Foundry Co. where they met with the conglomerate's lone security guard and saw the industrial site Bloxom had described. Rusted out boxcars, mechanical cranes, scrap metal crushers, and a junkyard surrounding a steel plant. Just about anyone could ditch just about anything here and it would never be seen again, nor viewed by human eyes on its way to the ravenous furnace. If Bloxom had been on assignment for Brock, and if he had carried in his hand a suitcase of guns used for a killing, and if he had swung that suitcase into one of the condemned boxcars, Brock could be satisfied that his orders had been well carried out. So much for finding the missing murder weapons in Alabama.

As for the envelope, Lloyd and Stearns paid a visit to what remained of Bloxom's family at their home on Twenty-eighth Avenue. One of Alexander Bloxom's three brothers, Roosevelt, last had possession of the envelope, if this whole convoluted story was to be believed. Officers already knew from their prison interview with Bloxom that Roosevelt had been murdered by a gang in Chicago on January 9, 1970, just a month before they visited Leavenworth. They also knew, from their own sources, that Roosevelt's apartment had been searched by Chicago police following his murder and that no envelope was found. Still, they wanted to find out what the family had done with Roosevelt's effects.

With one son dead and one in prison, Walter and Bessie Bloxom told the detectives that they had sent their two remaining sons, Walter Jr. and Willie, to Chicago to collect Roosevelt's possessions and see about the burial of their youngest. When the boys returned to Birmingham, they had with them all of Roosevelt's clothes and other belongings.

Of this meager estate, police wrote this in their report: "There were numerous papers and items that did not appear to have any value that they placed in a brown paper sack and left in the room. They stated that in these papers were some reels of tape and a sheet of paper with some phone numbers and instructions on it. They did not recall any specific names; however, they appeared to be Italian. These things were in an envelope at the time they looked at them." An aunt to the Bloxom boys said she might have thrown some papers in the garbage while she was doing her regular cleaning. From there, neither the papers, nor the reels of tape, nor the paper sack were ever seen again.

* * *

On March 2, 1970, Lyons and Stearns went to Michigan's Jackson Prison and interviewed Robert Matthews, the man Bloxom had said could have been Brock's accomplice in the Robison murders. Matthews was serving five to fourteen years on a conviction for uttering and publishing. That's a formal-sounding term for plain stealing but using fancy tactics. Yes, Matthews knew both Bloxom and Brock and yes, he was with them when the gas stations were robbed. No, he didn't kill the Robisons; he'd never been north of Flint in his life. He also volunteered his opinion of the character of both Brock and Bloxom: The former was ruthless enough to do such a crime and proud enough to brag about it; the latter wasn't smart enough to make up the kind of story the officers were now in the process of checking out. Yes, he'd take a polygraph.

* * *

On March 12, 1970, Robert Louis Matthews passed his polygraph test.

On March 16, 1970, officers Lyons and Stearns interviewed Ernest Gilbert, a former employee of Richard Robison, and learned that he owned a platinum silver 1965 Ford Thunderbird that he loaned to Joseph Scolaro on several occasions in June 1968.

On March 20, 1970, Detective Stearns interviewed Dave Miller, an inmate of Marquette Prison, serving time for parole violation. He stated that on June 24, 1968, he purchased a five-shot revolver in Toledo and that Mark Warren Brock couldn't have killed the Robisons because he was with Miller when he bought it.

On April 13, 1970, Alexander Bloxom failed his polygraph test.

* * *

The matter of the hapless bank robbers, the locked suitcase, the mysterious taped-up envelope, the secretive meeting at the fried chicken restaurant, and the Toledo gun-buying trip would probably have been put to rest when Alexander Bloxom failed his polygraph test—were it not for a nondescript dark blue Chevy later found abandoned on the side of a southern Michigan county road. The crime Bloxom professed to have knowledge of was submitted to the Kansas polygraph examiner as a case study, stated like this:

> The above person examined had submitted information to the effect that he knew who killed the Robison family. He indicated that one Robert Lewis Matthews and a Mark Brock had told him that they had been paid by a subject by the name of Scolaro or Scolatta. He further advised that the subject, Brock, had given him some checks with the name Richard C. Robison Co. printed on them. He was told to hold the checks for a possible extortion plot. He states he took the checks in question to his mother's home in Alabama.

With that, polygraph examiner Richard L. North went to Leavenworth Federal Penitentiary, hooked Bloxom up to his machine, and questioned him. Following the test, he had the option of grading Bloxom with a T for telling the truth, a D for deception, an I for indefinite results, an R for refusing to cooperate, or an O for other relating circumstances or for an incomplete test. Bloxom got a D. Deception.

"A post-test interview was conducted with negative results," North reported. "During the purpose portion of the interview there were discrepancies noted in his story."

Without any further cooperation from Brock or Matthews and with Bloxom's likely half-truths, inconsistencies, and even outright lies, there were no more tangents for police to follow on the Leavenworth letter theory, and that should have been the end of it. And it was, for more than four years. Then in late summer of 1973, a blue 1965 Chevy coach with Ohio license plates and something unexpected in the glove box was found abandoned by the side of M-14, a county road in southern Michigan.

The owners of the car could not be immediately located, and so it was towed to a local auto repair shop, where it sat unmolested for more than six months. By February 1974, enough time had gone by for the repair shop to assume ownership of the unclaimed vehicle, but not before a state trooper checked through it and added the vehicle identification number to his official report. That task fell to a Trooper Maxwell of the Romeo police post, and when he searched the car, he found a luggage tag bearing the name "Shirley L. Robison" and the address "18790 Dolores, Lathrup Village, Michigan" in the glove box. Recognizing the name as that of a now infamous murder victim, Maxwell called for backup and Detective Flis responded. The two searched the vehicle thoroughly, but no other evidence related to the murders was found.

Back at the Romeo post, police researched the Chevy's genealogy. Owned by a seemingly random series of blue-collar men and their uncles and sons and assorted hangers-on, the car had been originally purchased from Jim White Chevrolet in Toledo, on June 9, 1966.

It was the car's infancy in the city of Toledo that put officers in mind of the Leavenworth letter theory. The car was sold new off the lot in Toledo in 1966; Brock, possibly Bloxom, and Matthews had gone to Toledo in 1968 to buy guns; the Robisons were murdered a few weeks later; and then Shirley Robison's luggage tag was found in the car in 1974. A connection about as reliable as the mechanicals on the abandoned car itself, but enough, again, to set officers to the task of looking into the matter further.

Trooper Flis found that the car's title history included a Toledo trucking dispatcher and his uncle; a foreman for a glass company and his two teenagers, also from Toledo; a Toledo Ford dealership; a restaurant owner from Tawas, Michigan, his son, a blur of this son's "hippie type" friends; and finally a joy ride from Cedar Point Amusement Park in Ohio across the border to Michigan, where something like a cracked radiator took it down.

In the ensuing months, the trucking dispatcher and his relatives, the glass company foreman and his teenagers, the restaurant owner, his son, and the hodgepodge of hippies that could be located were all interviewed, and shown the luggage tag. Separately, each one said they had never seen the tag before and had no idea how or when it had been put in the Chevy's glove box. One of the hippie friends had stolen the car from Cedar Point and driven it until it broke down 120 miles later. He was found, interviewed, and, just like his comrades, could offer nothing further.

By this point the car was nine years old, the "new" piece of evidence was six years old, and by adding up relatives, friends, neighbors and car shoppers, a hundred people or more had probably driven the Chevy between the time it appeared on the new-car lot in Toledo and the time it broke down on the side of the county road in Michigan. Officers had no choice but to turn their attention elsewhere.

"To John Flis, the lead detective on the case, the luggage tag was a more vexing oddity than a breakthrough clue," stated a July 22, 1998, article in the *Oakland Press*.

The status of the once promising Leavenworth letter theory was the same now as the status of the case itself. Every lead had been followed down dusty southern roads, to the doorstep of a Chicago gang, over scrap metal yards, and inside the gloomy afternoon hours of jails and prisons, until those leads could be followed no further. The official police term for that status is *Complaint Remains Open*.

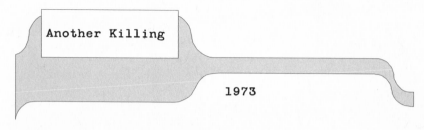

Another Killing

1973

Mother--where do I start . . .

—Joseph Scolaro, March 8, 1973

With no confession from Joe forthcoming, Stearns and Flis were deter-mined to find the missing murder weapons and they started with a search for the rifle. The detectives decided they would try a new tact in their search: using the media.

Two years had passed since Scolaro's check kiting arrest and their in-terrogation with him when he revealed that he had owned two AR-7s. A year and a half had passed since prosecutor Noggle not only declined to is-sue a warrant for their chief suspect but put forth his own theory instead. The missing rifle still hadn't been found, and the detectives contacted edi-tors at the *Detroit News* and enlisted their help. The newspaper ran an arti-cle in the June 27, 1971, Sunday edition of the paper about the still unsolved case, requesting that anyone with information about an Armalite .22-cal-iber long rifle A-7 Explorer please come forward.

"Some unsuspecting Michigan resident may now possess the gun," re-porter Joseph E. Wolff wrote in his article. Wolff went on to quote Cap-tain Daniel Myre, chief of detectives: "The killer may have dumped it in the woods somewhere, sold it or disposed of it in some way that it is now in someone else's hands. It is not a common type of weapon and is easily recognized, but the person who has it might have no idea it had been used in a mass slaying."

Captain Myre said they were looking for AR-7s purchased in the past three years. The *Detroit News* put up a $1,000 reward for information lead-ing to the recovery of the murder weapon.

After that article appeared, the proverbial woodwork split wide open. The first call was from a mother about her son, who was in the service over-seas. Mary Davis of Clarkston called the post and said that her twenty-one-year-old son, John, who was in the army and stationed in Germany, had bought a gun like the one described in the newspaper. He left it at home the last time he was on leave, and officers were welcome to it. Stearns and Flis went to her Allen Road home and picked up the weapon. No match.

Then a sergeant from Wurtsmith Air Force Base in Oscoda called to say he had an AR-7 and officers could test it if they were so inclined. They were, but no match.

The owner of the J & B Gun Shop of Petoskey called to say he had sold two AR-7s, both of which he had originally picked up at the Williams Gun Sight Company in Davidson. His customers were local men, and officers could check his records if they'd like. Both customers were tracked down and brought their guns to the store, where they were test-fired. The spent cartridges were sent to the crime lab. No match.

Officers on patrol or working cases around the state were advised to be on the lookout for AR-7s, and they obliged. Troopers in Bridgeport, East Tawas, Newberry, Grand Haven, North Muskegon, Gladstone, Plymouth, East Lansing, and Brighton all turned in AR-7s either confiscated from suspects in other crimes or volunteered by citizens. No matches. For a supposedly unusual weapon, there sure were a lot of them out there. Apparently Armalite, a California-based company, did a lot of business in Michigan.

Mrs. Harold Edgar of Saginaw wrote to Captain Myre that she and her husband had purchased such a gun at the Peters Gun Shop in Saginaw and police could check the gun at any time. And finally, another AR-7 was found in a motel room at the Elm Lodge Resort on M-55 in Houghton Lake. No matches. This model gun might indeed be rare; the specific one they were looking for, though, was even rarer, if it even still existed.

* * *

In the meantime, Joe continued to struggle financially. He tried to keep a low profile, but the detectives and an increased interest by the media following the article in the *Detroit News* made that increasingly difficult. He also continued to maintain his innocence.

"I've thought this over a lot," Joe told police during one of their final interviews with him. "I've thought the fact that somebody could have had revenge, trying to get them, you know, somebody as you said, it may be somebody's husband. I thought maybe an artist that Dick may have cut down to size and I've thought that it might have been a gang coming in. But I couldn't imagine anybody trying to touch Shirley or anybody else. A lot of things have gone through my mind, where it would be anything, you know?"

* * *

On the afternoon of May 8, 1973, Joe sent his mother out on an errand. He taped a handwritten note on the outside of the door, then tightly closed it behind him. He sat down at his desk in his high-back chair, put a piece of paper in his typewriter, and drafted another short note. He took the note out of the typewriter, signed it, added a postscript, and laid it on top of his desk. He took a Beretta handgun out of his desk drawer, loaded it with eight rounds of .25-caliber bullets, put it to his right temple, and pulled the trigger. The shot was what police call a "through-and-through"—in this case it passed through its victim's head and broke the glass in a picture hanging on the wall behind his desk.

The note on his office door read, "Mother—don't you come in—I will already be dead! Please have someone else come in—and you call the police or whatever. Joe."

The note on his desk read, "Mother—where do I start . . . I am a liar-cheat-phony. Any check that any of the people have with your signature isn't any good, because I forged your name to it to get them off my back. I owe everybody you can think of. I have made poor investments, and in some cases no investments at all. I love you dearly but living only causes you more heartache. I know I'm sick, but seeking help isn't going to help the people I've hurt. I just can't help myself . . . please understand. Love, Joe. P.S. I had nothing to do with the Robisons—I'm a cheat but not a murderer. Joe. I'm sick and scared—God and everyone please forgive me. I hope my family will understand."

While on the scene, officers looked through Joe's business files.

"It appeared that he was heavily in debt and was being pressured by various business associates to repay loans, etc.," they wrote in their report. This was just a general impression; they were unable to gauge the specifics of these debts and the exact nature of his business from the records, however. Their questioning of Joe's mother, Kitty, was of little help: "His mother displayed a rather hostile attitude to officers and no information could be obtained relative to the victim's business activities or everyday habits."

Besides the loaded gun and the fired .25-caliber slug they dug out of the wall, officers took the suicide notes, a ballpoint pen, and three typewriters from the office to be examined by the crime lab.

In just two weeks, they were supposed to be having a meeting with Ronald Covault, the chief assistant Oakland County prosecutor who had advised them more than three years ago that there was enough evidence to arrest Joe. His boss, L. Brooks Patterson, had been interested in the case as well. They were looking for a way to sidestep Noggle. If it could be proven that a conspiracy to commit murder had been hatched in Oakland County, even though it had been carried out up north, the Oakland County prosecutor would be well within the law to issue an arrest warrant. The rumor was that this is exactly what happened and Joe Scolaro got wind of it and killed himself rather than face a trial. With his body now in the care of the William R. Hamilton Funeral Home in Birmingham, however, the meeting was canceled.

Joseph Raymond Scolaro III, former Harvard University student, veteran of the Army Security Agency, gun hobbyist, salesman, beloved son, husband, and father of two young sons was dead by his own hand at the age of thirty-seven. For all intents and purposes, he had taken the investigation of the Robison murders along with him.

```
If that crime happened today, with the
resources we have now, it'd be solved,
no question.
```

—Sheriff Pete Wallin, in an interview in July 2007

It must have seemed like a good idea at the time. That and way too much beer are the only explanations Emmet County sheriff Pete A. Wallin can figure for why a local teenager would steal a backhoe at three o'clock in the morning on a Sunday and steer it down the middle of South Lakeshore Drive in Good Hart.

"Yeah, usually they pick something smaller. You know, like a car," the sheriff said.

The kid had just been to a party and was walking through the woods when, he told the sheriff, someone jumped him in the dark and then for no reason just beat him bloody. He didn't mean to steal the backhoe, he said, it was just there, the keys were in it, it was in the right place at the right time, and provided his most convenient means of escaping his assailant. A $2,500 bond and a stay in the Emmet County Jail was all that he escaped to, the sheriff noted.

Wallin grew up in Southfield, Michigan, coincidently the city next door to the Robisons' sheltered and more privileged Lathrup Village, but the sheriff has spent the entirety of his adult life in law enforcement in Emmet County. Though he's become accustomed to the shenanigans of intoxicated teenagers and protects what is largely a resort community, he's no stranger to the more serious crimes of arson, assault, and even first-degree murder.

In the winter of 2006, he and his deputies tracked down another man on the run, this one fully criminal, and not simply misguided by alcohol and drugs. Fugitive Stephen Grant, a wife killer, potentially armed and dangerous, was found by the sheriff and his men cowering under a fallen pine tree in a remote part of Wilderness State Park, about thirty miles north of Good Hart. Grant's wife had been missing for several days, and her torso had just turned up in an incriminating place — the couple's garage.

Wilderness State Park covers more than seven thousand acres of hiking paths, cross-country ski trails, campsites, and raw forest. The property is bordered by Big Sucker Creek to the south, Goose Bay to the west, the Straits of Mackinac to the north, and Carp River to the east. On a clear day from a campsite on the beach, you can see the Mackinaw Bridge. Wilderness Park is the single largest tract of undeveloped state land in Michigan's lower peninsula, hospitable to black bear, bald eagles, and even the endangered piping plover, but in early March no place for a man on the run without jacket, boots, gloves, or shelter.

It was fourteen degrees out and snowing hard when the officers found Grant, who was wearing just a shirt, pants, and socks, and listening to his own chattering teeth. He was shivering uncontrollably, was unarmed, and later confessed to strangling his wife in their Detroit-area home and dismembering her body. Two days earlier, Macomb County deputies had gone to the Grant home, searched it and found Tara Grant's torso. A teenager stealing a backhoe on a bender could be explained away, but the sheriff could offer no explanations for this crime, nor say why the man thought he could make his escape in the north.

"I don't care who you are or how bad you are or what you've done, you're still no match for the country up here unless you're prepared," Wallin said. "When we found him, he couldn't have lasted much longer."

When Wallin was about the same age as the backhoe thief, he enrolled in the criminal justice and law enforcement program at Ferris State University in Big Rapids. As a senior, he signed up for an internship with the Emmet County Sheriff's Office under then sheriff Richard L. Zink. Zink was in office when the Robisons were murdered, the crime happening during his watch, and Wallin remembers those days clearly. In 1968 the area was less populated, and the department consisted only of a sheriff, an undersheriff, a chief deputy, two jailers, and a secretary.

The Emmet County Sheriff's Office of today has separate divisions to deal with road patrol, corrections, animal control, and civil process; a dive team; marine and snowmobile patrols; as well as a staff of detectives and evidence technicians.

In the hours before Grant was apprehended, Macomb County Sheriff's Department detectives from the Detroit area drove north, partly because they questioned the ability of Emmet County to bring Grant in. By the time Grant was apprehended, though, they were giving their northern cohorts high fives, thanking them for a job well done. Wallin and his crew had used tracking dogs, a helicopter, and snowmobiles in the search. A confessed wife-killer roaming the woods is bound to attract media attention, and when all was said and done, it was Wallin the big-time reporters wanted to interview, not just the guys from urban Macomb County. The sheriff was quoted in *USA Today,* both of the Detroit dailies, on the three major television networks, plus Fox News, MSNBC, and CNN.

The operation to apprehend Grant had been flawless; the department was decades away from the days when former undersheriff Clifford Fosmore grabbed a paper towel, wrapped it around the handle of the bloody hammer used on the Robisons, and held it up so that a news reporter could snap a photograph, inadvertently wiping away any evidence the murderer might have left there.

"Things were pretty simple back then, and we didn't have the capability of dealing with a case like that," Sheriff Wallin said. "If that crime happened today, with the resources we have now, it'd be solved, no question."

Besides a staff well trained in handling evidence, the resources Sheriff Wallin has at his disposal that Sheriff Zink didn't have in 1968 include a gas chromatograph to perform chemical tests, rape kits to determine a sexual assault, detailed fiber analysis testing, evidence collection standards, crime scene photographing standards, and, of course, the grand tool of forensic science, DNA analysis. The DNA-testing capabilities that crime labs have today were developed in the 1980s, more than a decade after the Robisons were murdered.

"DNA testing revolutionized the field of forensic science practically overnight," writes criminalist John Houde in his book *Crime Lab: A Guide for Nonscientists.* "[A] few tiny cells can conclusively identify an individual out of everyone else on the earth. . . . This is bad news for guilty defendants and heaven-sent for innocent ones."

Though blood DNA was smeared throughout the Robison cottage—in the furniture's upholstery, on the walls, soaked into the pine plank floors, and on the victims' clothing—it played no role in the Robison murder investigation until Sheriff Wallin opened a closet door on a July day in 2002. His predecessor, friend, and mentor Jeffrey Bodzick had just died unexpectedly of a heart attack; Wallin was appointed to replace him and was cleaning out the office along with other department employees. There in the back of a closet was a box. When they pulled it out into the light and opened it up, they found hundreds of documents related to the unsolved Robison case.

"Every detective that's ever been with the department since the crime gets that case," Wallin said. "Right then I just thought, 'Well, I guess it's my turn to assign it.'"

And so one of his first acts as sheriff was to assign the case to Sheriff's

Detective Bobra Johnston, who began a detailed examination of the documents found in the closet, along with the whole file on the case—boxes and boxes and boxes stored in the department vault. She started with the remaining physical evidence, including the clothing of the victims, the autopsy reports, slides of hair and tissue and the shell casings from the murder weapons. Then she got to work on the rest of the case file. Without help, Detective Johnston would need a month or more just to read through everything, so Michigan State Police detective Gwen White was called in to assist. The two detectives, just kids when the murders were committed, came face to face with the same horror that had obsessed countless officers from both the Sheriff's Office and the Michigan State Police who had worked the case over the years.

"It was putrid," Detective Johnston told the *Petoskey News-Review.* "The original officers on the scene said they were met with a wall of flies."

After the two detectives had organized the file and begun to absorb what was in it, they scheduled a meeting with the heads of the DNA, fingerprint, and ballistics investigation departments at the Michigan State Police crime lab in Grayling. This same evidence that Johnston and White examined had been picked through and considered from all angles by countless detectives, crime scene investigators, lab technicians, and administrators over the years. But this time, there was something else, something overlooked but potentially valuable. Found within the pallet-sized block of documents, folders, reports, taped interviews and catalogued physical evidence were three unidentified pubic hairs taken off the body of Shirley Robison.

Who left microscopic pieces of himself inside the Robison cottage on the day of the murders forty years ago? Officers could not imagine that the killer could wreak the kind of bloody havoc that their long-ago colleagues found waiting for them inside that log-built retreat without leaving at least some small bit of his own biology behind. Sheriff Wallin said he was convinced that there was DNA at the crime scene left by at least seven people, one of whom was not named Robison. This seventh person did not die in the cabin but instead left unscathed, and under his own evil power, to walk free.

On that July day in 2002, as he was just getting acclimated to his new title of duly appointed sheriff, Wallin thought that maybe, just maybe, the case could finally be closed, the manhunt that had gone on for decades, ever since he was a green college intern, could finally be over, and on his watch, no less.

At issue were the three pubic hairs, labeled evidence 2-D, found on Shirley's body that, upon visual inspection, had not looked to investigators like they came from any member of the Robison family. 2-D had been stored for more than thirty-four years in an ancient glass screw-top evidence collection jar sealed with cellophane tape. Johnston wanted the Michigan State Police Forensic Science Division to check the hairs against those collected from Shirley's family and to check for DNA evidence. The Robisons' blood-stained clothes were also to be checked. If DNA were found, its particular characteristics could be entered into a national database to look for a match—and the killer.

"Compare hair samples collected from victims to 3 pubic hairs (2-D) removed from Shirley Robison," Johnston wrote in her official request. "We sent down all of the hair evidence and Shirley's clothing. Gook luck and thanks."

Before the lab work was started, money, and a lot of it, happened to become available for tests on old DNA evidence. In March 2003, the Forensic Science Division received a $1.4 million federal grant to conduct DNA testing on cold cases. The grant allowed the Grayling laboratory to select 175 cases from around the state in which there were "existing biological samples" and to test them. The idea behind the grant was that these biological samples would be entered into CODIS (Combined DNA Indexing System), the national crime-fighting DNA database, and checked against existing records. Adding 175 new cases would also expand the scope of the database itself.

Johnston recontacted the state police and requested that the evidence she had submitted for analysis along with Shirley's clothing be included in the DNA analysis that the new grant was funding.

With this physical evidence now safely in the hands of a state police forensic scientist, Johnston turned her attention to the rest of the file. Among the most recent items in it were a series of letters written by a Davidson, Michigan, woman to the sheriff's office, the office of the prosecuting attorney, and the state attorney general's office. A letter with a similar story had been received by Davidson City Police and Flint Area Crime Stoppers.

The correspondent's bizarre story went like this: As an unwilling and hypnotized victim, she had been forced to witness the murders of the Robisons. The killers were two women sharpshooters from Traverse City, Michigan, who the woman believed were her friends. Her father, a Detroit-area psychiatrist, had helped orchestrate the crime and was waiting in a nearby cabin when it happened. A wide assortment of people connected to the case, including the Bliss family, various detectives, and the shooters themselves had been her father's patients. A police cover-up had kept the case from being solved for the past thirty-five years and now supported the harassment the correspondent was subjected to by unknown enemies. Her car and apartment were bugged, she said, and two frightening men had moved into her apartment building.

"Can you help me in spite of corrupt police who will try to convince you I'm crazy?" the woman wrote in one of her letters. "I receive Social Security Disability for anxiety disorder, which is not a psychosis. It's the result of extreme abuse, but I've earned, with hard work, a lot of healing with God's help. If you don't help me, I will not survive much longer. They want me dead, and they work at it."

Bobra Johnston hardly knew how to respond to this correspondent, who turned out to be just one in a very long line of people with outlandish theories on the crime. She was obviously disturbed; in twenty-one pages of correspondence she had reiterated the same preposterous story. And yet she was also obviously suffering and in need of the help she was requesting. Ultimately, Johnston referred the woman to her local police chief, William Brandon, and after the end of May received no more letters from her.

Johnston then turned her attention to a reexamination of the murder weapons, and found good news and bad news. The good news was that another division of the same state police forensic science lab that was looking for DNA confirmed the long-ago ballistics report. The shell casings at the cottage did match the shell casings found at a downstate firing range. The bad news was that there was no record of the gun ever being used again in the intervening three-plus decades; it was still good and missing.

In June 2003 the DNA forensic work on the three mysterious hairs and Shirley's disintegrating clothing had been completed. The news was not what the Sheriff's Office had been hoping to hear. The hairs did not have enough material attached for DNA analysis and neither did Shirley's clothing. When the "gross morphological characteristics" of the three hairs were examined under a microscope, they were determined to be similar to the known sample submitted from Shirley. All these years, many had assumed that Shirley had been raped, adding another dimension to the crime, to the investigation, and to the psyche of the person who had committed it. Now that the hair analysis was complete, detectives saw that Shirley may not have been raped, but that the killer had positioned her body to make it look as if she had.

Sheriff Wallin, even five years later, makes no effort to disguise his disappointment in the DNA test. "It was a long shot," he said, "but at least it *was* a shot."

2007

There is just something about this
case. Once you know a little bit about
it, you want to know more. No, you
don't just want to know more, you have
to know more. It's like it's
contagious, and what you catch from it
is obsession.

> —Emmet County detective J. L. Sumpter, in an
> interview, October 4, 2007

Aldred Koski is a yeller. An operation that removed part of his lung years ago has given the eighty-year-old man an angry wheeze. Lugging around an anchor of a briefcase, boxes of files and cassette tapes of interviews, a camera, a tape recorder, and a laptop—elements of his "roving office of incrimination" according to another reporter—probably hasn't helped his respiration any, either. These materials, though, are both the treasure and detritus of nearly four decades of meticulous investigative reporting, and they have traveled with him in his van as he's tracked the killer of the Robisons over umpteen Michigan miles.

Ask questions about the investigation of any number of people with a stake in its outcome—Sheriff Wallin, Detective Sumpter, author Judith Guest, Petoskey newspaper editor Kendall Stanley, for example, and they'll eventually steer you to Koski. Former Emmet County detective Bobra Johnston credits him with keeping the case alive. Retired state police detective John Flis kept a scrapbook of Koski's articles and once told him, "You really dogged it good." High praise from a cop to a reporter. Koski, they say, has compiled more information on the crime than anyone else, possibly even law enforcement. The man said as much himself in a September 18, 2007, e-mail:

> I spent $1,000 on converting 10,000 feet of Robisons' home
> movies into DVDs. From that I know the mannerisms of the kids

. . . How tall Richard Craig was. What they visited in San Francisco. What were the views they had from the Delta air coach as the family came in view of the Hawaiian Islands? I can describe perfect sunsets and kids splashing in the water. These same kids opening up gifts at Christmas and the frosting on birthday cakes. It only took me 38 years to reach this point. What I've put down on paper here barely scratches the surface.

Shirley Robison's brother, Marvin Fulton, gave Koski the Robison family home movies once he'd established his interest in helping to solve the case. Other gems in his stash include some of Dick Robison's financial records that Koski found inside a file cabinet he picked up for ten dollars at an IRS tax sale; photographs of the inside of the Robison cottage just days before it was torn down and burned; and tape recordings of interviews with people once close to the case but now long dead, such as Monnie Bliss, his parents, Chauncey and May Bliss, and even the state police's chief suspect, the enigmatic Joe Scolaro.

Koski is also the consummate beat reporter and can turn down the volume and the vitriol and just listen when it's needed to get a story. In his files are clips bearing his byline from the *Dearborn Press, Dearborn Guide, Detroit Times, Detroit Free Press, Oakland Press, Petoskey News-Review,* Reuters, and United Press International. His name appears in the Michigan State Police files on the case, and he turned over some of his records and notes to the Emmet County Sheriff's Office in the event some nugget of information buried inside could help solve the case.

He is quoted in many anniversary-themed articles that have appeared on schedule in Michigan newspapers as the unsolved crime has passed the twenty, twenty-five, thirty, and thirty-five-year mark. Koski's now-raspy voice also brought news of the investigation to radio listeners in the 1960s, most notably in his two part series, *The Six Who Died,* which aired on WKNR in 1969.

"You know when I hear those voices . . . [they] ring clear and in listening anew it sends chills up and down my spine almost as if I was resurrecting the dead," Koski wrote in another e-mail.

When the crime was discovered in July 1968, Detroit was in the throes of a newspaper strike. Trade unions at the city's two biggest dailies, the *Detroit Free Press* and the *Detroit News,* had banded together and called a strike in late November 1967, and neither paper published again until early August 1968. By then, the Robison crime had been known for two weeks, and readers around the state were starved for in-depth news of the investigation. Working at a small weekly newspaper, the *Dearborn Guide,* Koski recognized the news value in the case and tried to fill the void with as many articles as his superiors would publish. After the dailies started up again and his newspaper wouldn't fund him on a trip to the scene of the crime, Koski quit his job and headed north on his own dime.

"Eight months into the thing I heard the cabin was being torn down," Koski says. "What the hell? How are you going to bring a jury up there and get yourself a conviction?"

As early as the last week of August 1968, both the Emmet County Sheriff's Office and the Michigan State Police had informed the staff at the National Bank of Detroit that they had no more use for the property. "I spoke with Detective Stearns yesterday, who advised that neither he nor the State Crime Lab have any further investigative need for the property," Dean R. Luedders of the Real Estate Division of the National Bank of Detroit wrote to Undersheriff Clifford Fosmore on August 27, 1968. "Since Sheriff Zink advised last Friday that your office also wants no further responsibility specifically in connection with the property, we will assume responsibility for its supervision henceforth."

Perhaps it was the way evidence was collected in 1968 or how crime scenes were managed, or perhaps it was pressure from the neighbors who had said in no uncertain terms that they wanted the cottage torn down. Whatever the reason, as early as five weeks after the bodies were discovered, there were plans afoot to be rid of the log and stone structure that had encased the Robison family. Official plans were under way by February 1969.

Koski didn't have any idea exactly where the remote cottage was, but he felt compelled to at least try to see the inside of the place before a wrecking crew demolished it forever. And so, in the winter of 1969, he and his father drove the three hundred miles north and sought out Summerset. It wasn't an easy place for him to find, underscoring the early assertion of Sheriff Richard Zink that the killer must have been to the cottage at least once before. Tucked between Little Traverse Bay and a wooded bluff, well out of sight from the closest strip of asphalt, the spot is even more remote in the middle of winter. Before he finally found it, Koski, a small man, had trudged through snow as deep as his waist and was soaked through his gray suit and long black topcoat. Later, according to Koski, when he knocked on the front door of what turned out to be Chauncey Bliss's house, the elder Bliss would take one look at the reporter and say he looked like he had "arrived on a sled pulled by a dog team."

The weather conditions and Koski's impractical city duds didn't deter him from squeezing through an open bathroom window at the Robison cottage some previous visitor had left ajar. Once inside the main room, what he saw when he looked down was still horrific months after the crime.

> [I] glimpsed the jagged outline of Shirley Robison's corpse embedded in . . . the grain of the wood. In the photograph I took you can make out that the image is headless, cutoff at the knees, legs spread, pubic hair showing as a black smudge. Clear as well is her raised fist, which I viewed as her dying declaration of being utterly helpless to save her family and herself from the marauding son-of-a-bitch gunning them down in cold blood.

For nearly forty years the image in that photograph has fueled Koski's investigative engine, powering it still as he works on his own book about the case that, he says, is "a classic in the making." He has his own theory about the identity of the murderer and ridicules someone who would dare deviate from that idea, even novelists writing fiction. Mention fictionalized versions of the Robison story, and that's when the yelling starts again—these kinds of writers are just "muddying the waters!"

Despite Koski's fury, two novels have been inspired by the case: the self-published *Dead End* by James Pecora and *The Tarnished Eye* by widely acclaimed author Judith Guest (who also wrote the best-selling book, *Ordinary People,* which was later made into an Oscar-winning movie starring Mary Tyler Moore, Donald Sutherland, Timothy Hutton, and Elizabeth McGovern).

Guest, who says she's still intrigued by Sheriff Hugh DeWitt, the fictional main character she created for *The Tarnished Eye,* is working on a sequel to the mystery because as a writer she "really liked her sheriff and just couldn't let him go yet." The unpublished sequel, *White in the Moon,* takes its title from an A. E. Housman poem and opens seven years after DeWitt solves the murder of the Norbois family. The surname Norbois is a rearrangement of the letters in *Robison,* a diversion Guest unknowingly has in common with Dick Robison. Robison himself played around with the letters in his name, and on the masthead of several issues of *Impresario* listed the imaginary Carl R. Nosibor as art director.

"The murders had been on my mind for years and years," says Guest, a native of Detroit and graduate of the University of Michigan. "When I decided to write about it, I decided I didn't just want to write a novel, I wanted to solve the case."

As part of her research, Guest met with Koski. By coincidence, each was spending a few weeks one summer in their respective cottages not too far from Lake Huron in the northeastern part of the state. Guest was in Harrisville and Koski in Oscoda. He invited her over for a visit, she accepted, and was flabbergasted by the amount of research material he had brought along on vacation. Videotapes of news programs, audiotapes of radio programs, police files, transcribed interviews, personal letters and photographs, all pertaining to the case.

"It's fiction, Al," she told him several times when he wanted to discuss the minutia of the case and how her book deviated from his own research. "Al, it's fiction."

The Tarnished Eye was inspired not just by the Robison case, but also by another famous Michigan crime, the Co-Ed Murders. For two years, from July 1967 through July 1969, seven young women were murdered in Washtenaw County. The youngest was thirteen, the oldest twenty-three. Some were students at the University of Michigan, some at Eastern Michigan University, some still in junior high or high school. John Norman Collins, a sometime EMU student, was suspected in the murders and ultimately convicted, in 1970, of killing an eighteen-year-old EMU freshman named Karen Sue Beineman. He was sentenced to life in prison, has since changed his name to John Chapman, and is currently incarcerated behind razor wire, an electronic detection system, and eight gun towers in the Marquette Branch Prison, on the shore of Lake Superior in Michigan's Upper Peninsula.

What caught Guest's writer's eye was that John Norman Collins, aka John Chapman, was an acquaintance of Richard Craig Robison; the two met in 1967 when they both attended Eastern Michigan University and may have either roomed together during orientation for freshmen and new students (Collins had transferred as a sophomore from Central Michigan University) or been members of the same fraternity.

To add to the coincidence, although police had had their sights on him for weeks, Collins was finally arrested after housesitting for his uncle, David Leik, a Michigan state trooper. Leik was not involved in the Co-Ed Murders investigation, but he and his family had been on vacation and had enlisted Collins to feed their dog and check on their house while they were gone. When they returned, they found certain things amiss in their basement; drops of a dark liquid had dried on the floor and a can of paint, a box of laundry detergent, and a bottle of ammonia were missing. A crime lab crew found hair clippings and bloodstains in Leik's basement that tied Collins to Beineman, and he was arrested, tried, and convicted of the crime.

Years later, Leik was promoted to lieutenant and then was made commander of the Petoskey post. When he retired from the police force, he moved further north and served for a time as interim township supervisor for West Traverse Township, which borders on, of all possible places, neighboring Redmond Township and the village of Good Hart.

"What are the chances that this family knew this guy and he was not their killer?" Guest asks.

"Irrelevant," Koski would probably answer.

The state police did check into a possible link with Collins but could find nothing that would tie him to the Robison murders. A handwritten note from the Emmet County Sheriff's Office records reads, "Phone call with Stearns and Flis. They advise they can find no connection between Collins and the Robison boy, other than they went to the same school." Acquaintances of both told the police the boys knew each other but differed in recounting details of their introduction.

Koski covered Collins' preliminary court exam and observed nothing in common in the two crimes. Sheriff Zink and Lloyd Stearns conferred on the matter, comparing notes to see if the two investigations had turned up any names in common or if Collins had ever visited Summerset. Nothing was found and Collins has said little to the media or to police since his sentencing hearing in August 1970, when he maintained his innocence. At both his sentencing and in his only public interview since that time, Collins said that not only didn't he kill the young woman, he didn't even know anyone named Karen Sue Beineman.

Another sleuth in the case, known also to Guest and Koski, is a curious man by the name of Tom Mair. Guest and Mair share the belief that Collins could very well be the killer, or at least that the theory should be more thoroughly investigated by police. "If I was in front of a bunch of judges, I could make a case that he did it," Mair says. "You at least talk to him. You don't ignore him."

A former waiter and the manager of a movie theater in Traverse City, Mair was a neighbor of the Robisons on Dolores Street in Lathrup Village, and he was a childhood friend of Randy Robison, the youngest Robison boy. Randy was just twelve years old when he was murdered, a small boy for his age, shy and "cautious" according to the family's minister, Reverend Peters. "He was not as open in class and was withdrawn and a loner," Peters would later tell investigators. "He was very courteous—extremely courteous—and very quiet."

Close in age to Randy, Mair was devastated by the crime. He still has clear memories of the two boys riding their bikes and working on their

stamp collections together. Adding to his shock, he says, was the sentiment, "There but for the grace of God go I." Mair says he had been invited
to accompany the Robison family on their June trip to Summerset but
went on vacation with his own family instead.

The unlikely alliance between the movie theater manager and the
best-selling author came about in a Traverse City restaurant when Guest
was visiting on a book tour for *The Tarnished Eye*. Koski, meanwhile, fumes
over the idea and has called Mair's involvement in the case "fakery."

"Mair, trying to be ever so suave, tagged John Norman Collins as the
killer," Koski wrote in an August 16, 2007 e-mail. "He cashed in during a re-
gretful lull of our trusted news media; tired by then of the story and gave it
scant coverage in the passing years. Mair was able to plant his own version
of the whodunit . . . that the cops got it wrong in preaching that JRSIII
(Joseph R. Scolaro) killed them all."

Mair's father was either a union carpenter or steelworker (both stories
have circulated). His union was on strike that summer, and so the Mair
family decided to go camping together, sparing Tom the awful fate that be-
fell the Robisons. It is curious, however, that the Robisons would have invited an extra person along if they were planning to go to Kentucky and
Florida.

As a child, Mair felt powerless to do anything but express frustration
over the fact that no one had been punished for the crime. As a teenager, he
continued to think about it and finally went to see a Southfield, Michigan,
judge for advice on how he could help, though the visit ultimately led him
nowhere.

Still, the unsolved case would not leave him. In 1991, when Mair was an
adult, he contacted the Emmet County sheriff's office, and then in 1994
the Michigan State Attorney General's office, requesting that they take another look at Collins. Mair even found out where Dick Robison's sister,
Elaine Fox, lived and wrote her a letter. "I'm writing to you so that I may
have an opportunity to speak to a member of the Robison Family," he said.
"I would like to meet you at your convenience. I'd like to share some of my
thoughts on what happened to Shirley and her family. Perhaps you would
share your thoughts with me. If you prefer not to speak with me then
could you please refer me to another family member. Please take your time
in deciding your response."

Elaine Fox not only declined to meet with Mair, she called Detective
Stearns about the letter and then mailed a copy of it, along with her own
correspondence on a sheet of hearts and flowers stationery, to then Emmet County sheriff, Jeffrey Bodzick.

"A week ago I received this letter," she wrote to Bodzick. "It was a little upsetting. After 26 years, why now? I will not be contacting Mr. Mair."

By 1996, though, Mair had retained the services of a Birmingham attorney to push his cause with the attorney general. Frank Kelley's office took the tip seriously and assigned it to the Criminal Division for follow-up, but nothing was found in Mair's research to move the investigation forward.

"This is in reply to your recent letter requesting that this office investigate the Robison family murders which occurred in Good Hart in 1968," an attorney working in the Criminal Division wrote to Mair's attorney in March 1996. "You base your request on the fact that your client, Thomas Mair, has found evidence which indicates a possible connection between these homicides and John Norman Collins. Based on my review of the materials you provided, it appears that this connection was known at least back in 1970. Your letter does not contain any new evidence which would warrant any investigation by this office."

Still, Mair carried on. He contacted Grand Rapids Silent Observer, one of the Michigan branches of a national citizen's crime fighting group, and in 1998 convinced the organization to offer a $2,500 reward for any information that would lead to an arrest in the case. News of the reward generated about a dozen new anonymous tips pointing the finger at everyone from "an important hostess" in Detroit to one of Jimmy Hoffa's bodyguards, but none of the tips panned out. That same year, Mair helped initiate a meeting between the Emmet County Sheriff's Office, Emmet County Prosecutor's Office, Michigan Attorney General's Office, and the Michigan State Police.

A local weekly in Mair's adopted town of Traverse City, the *Northern Express,* got wind of his involvement in the investigation and interviewed him for an article that appeared in the paper's September 15, 1998, edition. He laid out his theory on the killer. "[I]t would have taken somebody with a mindset different than the caretaker and the business partner. My theory is that it was somebody with more of a criminal history—someone who is the worst example of a human being. Someone who doesn't just kill one person, but kills six and could be particularly violent towards a young girl."

According to the article, Mair feared for his own safety because of what he knew about the crime, but was nevertheless still gratified to see that his work had kept the case alive. In August 2004, he wrote his own first-person piece for the *Northern Express,* touting Guest's book and again naming John Norman Collins as his prime suspect in the Robison murders.

Mair and Guest had, in different times and for different reasons, come to the same conclusion before they had ever met at that Traverse City book-signing; despite whatever evidence the police had that pointed to Scolaro, they both agreed that convicted murderer John Norman Collins could not be ignored.

"I believe that in cases of this type the largest problem for law enforcement may be getting over the possibility that the original theory and prime suspect are wrong," Mair wrote in his piece in the *Northern Express,* titled "On the Trail of a Killer."

Guest's novel, Mair said in his article, might be just the thing to initiate a new look at the old case, and maybe even focus on a new suspect. There was a flush of media attention about the case that appeared in newspapers around Michigan coinciding with the release of Guest's book and the thirty-fifth anniversary of the crime. Mair said he expects the same thing when the fortieth anniversary rolls around.

"I plan on stirring up stuff," he said. "Stirring up tips."

The Good People
of Good Hart

2007

If one would enjoy to the fullest
extent the beauties of nature, he
should drive over Shore Drive between
Harbor Springs and Cross Village. I
rarely pass over these 21 miles that I
am not constrained to say with [Sir
Walter] Scott, "Breathes there a man
with soul so dead, who never to
himself has said This is my own, my
native land."

—Retired judge and amateur forester John J. Gafill,
in *American Forests,* June 1962

In 1968 Good Hart was, and today still is, a mythical place, a magical land, a place where J. R. R. Tolkien could have imagined Middle Earth, or C. S. Lewis could have conjured his Narnian woods. Robin Hood, Tarzan, Amelia Earhart, and the boy from *My Side of the Mountain* could stride out of the forest together and walk into the Good Hart General Store to shop for provisions, and chances are good that no one would act all that surprised. Before the murders inside Summerset cottage, Sir Thomas More could have set his *Utopia* along Shore Road and, with its idyllic and remote coastline, the geography would have made a fitting locale.

All the elements for a good fairy-tale are here: dark woods, warm cabins with smoke curling from their chimneys, worn footpaths down ancient routes, watery blue-gray horizons, a church, a graveyard, and a little store. Not to mention the resident Odawa Indian spirits.

While no one has ever reported seeing a ghost at the site of the Robison cottage, it has an uncanny stillness, and the site remains undeveloped. Just south, an evil spirit is said to haunt Devil's Elbow, a ravine that juts like a war wound off the winding asphalt. Steve Shananaquet's common-law wife, Agnes, said her ancestors heard "voices and sounds" echoing out from this ravine after nightfall. If the Devil's Elbow doesn't get you, the Indian

Drum might, locals say, with a mixture of delight and caution. The deep booming of a huge drum is said to beat across this land when anyone dies in or near the unpredictable waters of Little Traverse Bay.

"None of the local residents recalls hearing the drum in late June when the Robisons were murdered," reported the *Petoskey News-Review* a week after the crime. "But neither did anyone hear the fusillade of shots which claimed their lives."

The legends of sprits roaming around Shore Drive go back at least as far as a famous lacrosse game played just beyond the gates of Fort Michilimackinac on a hot June afternoon in 1763. Chief Pontiac had led his rebellion against the British in Detroit a month before and Indian uprisings were reported at military and trading outposts throughout the state. At the northern tip of Michigan's Lower Peninsula, an Englishman by the name of Captain George Etherington was in charge of forty-odd soldiers at Fort Michilimackinac. On June 2, 1763, he and his charges watched as a visiting tribe of Sauk challenged the Odawa to a game of lacrosse.

Captain Etherington ignored a local fur trader who had warned him that the Odawa men were just as capable of an attack as the dreaded Chief Pontiac. While the Odawa men flipped their fire-charred wooden ball around the outside of the fort with their sticks, the soldiers' muskets sat idle and unloaded, and the gates of the fort were pushed all the way open for a better view of the athletes.

The Sauk and Odawa women came to watch the game too, wearing blankets wrapped tightly around their shoulders like shawls, even though the day had turned hot and humid. When one of the players flipped the ball over the fort's wall, seemingly by accident, the Odawa women opened their blankets, and the lacrosse players grabbed the weapons hidden inside them and attacked. Seventeen British soldiers were killed in the fight, and the Odawa held the fort for an entire year.

"The dead were scalped and mangled, the dying were writhing and shrieking under the knife and tomahawk," wrote one witness to the attack. Local legend has it that the seventeen soldiers killed that day are the owners of the "voices" heard by Agnes Shananaquet's forebears. Whether the six members of the Robison family have added their own cries to the legend, no one can say.

There has been a church here engaged in holy battle against such superstitions since 1741, more than twenty years before the Fort Michilimackinac massacre and two hundred years before the Robisons. The French Jesuits built it, then abandoned it in the 1760s when the British established their claim over much of Michigan and the New World. The

British were not as faithful as the French, and the church fell into decline until after the Revolutionary War. By the 1830s, Father Baraga, "the snowshoe priest," was walking across the frozen crust of the northern Midwest and igniting a Catholic fervor from Wisconsin through the Upper Peninsula of Michigan and down to Good Hart. So inspired were the Odawa by his faith, that they built an addition onto St. Ignatius to house his growing flock. By the time Father Baraga blessed it on August 1, 1833, he counted 1,842 souls saved, 547 of which had been rescued in the course of his own missions. Father Baraga is up for canonization for his sincere spiritual efforts, despite the hardships of the local geography.

"The territory of Michigan, which includes the region of Arbre Croche, is a country very sparsely inhabited, especially in the vicinity of my mission station," he wrote in a letter to his sister, Amalia, dated March 8, 1832. "The interior of the country is mountainous and entirely desolate, nothing but a forest and entirely uninhabited; only the shores of the extremely great Lake Michigan are inhabited. This extensive forest, which has a greater area than all of the empire of Austria is entirely uninhabited and serves the Indians for the chase."

In time, some of the souls Baraga and other missionaries saved went on to their heavenly reward, and so a graveyard was parceled out to the south of the church, now called St. Ignatius Mission Church. The oldest date on any of the gravestones is 1855, marked for someone named Nebawkwin, though the church's current caretaker is certain that it is downright new compared to the dates of some of the unmarked graves.

If there is a better place to spend eternity, it would be difficult to imagine where it would be. Today, this quiet wooded place resembles a mossy, lichen-covered, woodsy miniature Arlington. Lines of freshly painted white crosses undulate up the hill toward the forest beyond. Sun shines directly on the front doors of the church, making the building seem to glow. The pom-pom of hydrangea bushes planted along the fieldstone foundation in the fall of 2007 look as if they're going to take.

"No one will ever know the true age and identity of all of the people buried here, and I'll tell you why," says Stephanie Guyor, St. Ignatius restoration coordinator and all-around good neighbor. "They didn't put names on when they were buried all those centuries ago. They decorated them just so, just beautifully, with ornate iron crosses and wreaths of flowers, but no names and no dates."

Stephanie, a petite redhead who retired to Good Hart after years of loyal work as a guidance counselor downstate in Grand Blanc, pulls up to the church in her red two-seater convertible, ignoring the brisk October chill. She is in charge of making sure the sanctuary is opened every morning and closed every evening from May through October. She and her husband, Richard, have marshaled local money, labor, and devotion, making the St. Ignatius Preservation Fund a great success.

The little mission church has a new steeple with stained glass windows, a new well and septic system, new squirrel-proof wiring, a new roof and fresh paint, inside and out. When the hanging lights crafted years ago by a class of fifth-graders from Harbor Springs were missing some colored marbles, she went shopping on eBay to replace them. A refurbished organ is coming, and so is a remodeled room where retired priests can enjoy a summer-long respite—and conduct a few masses. As it is now, the only services are the Sunday before and after the Fourth of July holiday.

The Guyors bought property here in the 1960s, and Monnie Bliss was one of the first people they met in the area. It was wintertime and they had driven north to check the progress on the building of their cottage. Snow that year had fallen and fallen and then fallen some more until the total was close to a new record. A huge snowbank blocked the road between town and their property, and the Guyors had to turn around and head back home without reaching their destination. On their way, they passed Monnie going the opposite direction in his plow truck. Both vehicles slowed, and windows were rolled down.

Stephanie recalls, "We said hello and then asked if we could hire him to plow us out. He said, 'I don't plow for money, I plow for love. Once I get to know you, maybe I'll plow for you and maybe I won't.'"

The Guyors liked him instantly, and both Stephanie and Richard became good friends with Monnie. He could build, invent, or fix just about anything, Stephanie marveled. When Richard accidentally broke into splinters a wooden ladder that had been his father's, Monnie carefully gathered up the pieces, told Richard not to worry, and went to his workshop. A few days later, he returned with the ladder, its condition more secure than before it had broken.

"That meant a lot to my husband because his father had just died and so it wasn't just some old thing. It had sentimental value," Stephanie says. "That was just the kind of thing he did for people. It was more than thirty years ago now, and can you believe it, we're still using that ladder."

In an endearing way, Monnie called Stephanie "his psychiatrist," because of her counseling background. He would call her on the phone or drive by her cottage and say, "I need to talk to my psychiatrist," chuckling. The two talked often, she says, about both trivial matters and important issues. Monnie had an active mind and was a constant worker, skilled in everything from cutting ice out of the bay, to forecasting the weather, to forging handmade iron hardware, to building his log cottages from the ground up, to publishing a little mimeographed newsletter.

The *Driftwood Journal* was mailed out in the winter months to summer people at their downstate winter addresses. Monnie had a goofy sense of humor that often came through in his writing. "The snow over along the shore is less than knee deep except where it drifted," Monnie wrote in the January 1959 issue. "Over in the Sogonoah Valley where I live, it is knee deep if you stand on your head."

Monnie died of kidney failure between Christmas and New Year's Eve in 1980, when he was sixty-nine. He had suffered from kidney disease for many years, and the progression of the illness made sleep difficult. Sometimes, his speech would be slurred and his thinking slowed. As Sheriff Wallin puts it, "He got odd at the end."

Stephanie says it makes her sad to think that the side effects of a debilitating illness caused people who didn't know her friend to consider him a suspect in the Robison murders. "People like being with their own thoughts when they come here to the church. I know I do, and sometimes I even think about Monnie," Stephanie says. "Anyone can come here and sit, relax, think, and pray. There's a certain serenity to this kind of oasis out in nature."

A half-mile south lives another longtime Good Hart summer resident. Virginia "Ginny" Taylor is ninety-four years old, a widow, and has been coming to Good Hart from Ohio since she was a teenager. She remembers May Bliss's delicious chicken dinners served family style at Blisswood's Krude Kraft Lodge and neighborhood beach parties at Talbot's Heights beach. She too remembers Monnie. He built the cottage Ginny and her husband retired in, and for a little while, before she got married, Monnie was her sweetheart.

"He was a couple years older than me, but I was smitten with all the things he knew about nature," she says. "We would walk though the woods, and he would point out a group of maple trees growing close together that were tapped in the spring for maple syrup and say, 'That's a sugarbush.' Then he'd make sure I noticed a particularly pretty grove of birch trees. Those were the things that were important to him. If we walked in the woods at night, he knew his way so well, he didn't need a flashlight. He'd tell me not to be afraid. That the woods were beautiful, and not frightening."

One spring, a month before she was to come north to Good Hart for the summer, a package arrived in the mail from Monnie. She set it on the kitchen table, and when she opened it, the smell of the northern woods filled the whole room. Inside were live arbutus plants, their roots buried in two inches of sandy northern Michigan soil. Arbutus is a delicate wildflower native to Good Hart and the surrounding area that blooms for only a few days every spring.

"They were blooming," Virginia says. "Isn't that just something?"

A Bliss House

2007

> Greetings once again from the
> beautiful land of your vacation, the
> home of the Sidehill Gougers and Half
> Pint Pete. We begin our second year of
> the Journal hoping that you have not
> forgotten us and that you have
> forgiven us the sins of the past year.
> The summer seemed pretty short,
> didn't it?
>
> —Monnie Bliss, *Driftwood Journal,* October 1959

Summerset was a Bliss house. The term is used to describe not the outlook of the inhabitants within but rather the architecture and materials of the structure itself. Chauncey P. Bliss developed the log-style home out of solid logs from trees felled in the area, fieldstones collected along the shore or dug out of the hillside for the foundation and fireplace, hand-hewn beams overhead, and built-in furniture below. Decorative exterior touches made of twigs and birch or elm bark make each home unique.

The Bliss family's best guess is that all together, during the years from about 1930 until about 1970, Chauncey and his son Monnie built between thirty and forty of the homey cottages, many of which remain treasured retreats by their owners to this day. Monnie Bliss died in 1980, but in the preceding months he told his oldest daughter, Bonnie Bliss Weitzel, that he wanted to document his life's work before he died. He created a list of each of the cottages he'd built, the year each was constructed, and the names of the owners he'd built it for.

Besides being a creative man and talented builder, Monnie was also a good salesman. In the late 1950s and early 1960s he published a little mimeographed newsletter, the *Driftwood Journal,* that he mailed out in the winter months to people who vacationed or owned property in and around Blisswood.

"We hope that the New Year is good to you and that all you ladies will give your husbands a new cottage for a birthday present," he wrote in the January 1959 issue. "Remember ladies . . . we build 'em!"

In March of the same year he wrote, "It's getting to be about time that some of you folks started thinking of getting back here. We miss you a lot and would like to build you a new cottage or an addition to your present one."

When Monnie died, the paper listing his building accomplishments disappeared in the shuffle, and Bonnie Bliss said that sadly, no one knows for sure how many Bliss cottages were built and how many of those are still standing. Though some have been preserved, many others have been re-modeled so drastically that their current owners might not even know that they own one.

Most of the Bliss cottages are within a few miles of Good Hart, cen-tered around Lamkin Drive, within the Blisswood resort development it-self, or on South Shore Drive. Some have names, or did at one time, like the Robisons' Summerset, or The Pebble, Timber Bend, or the Weitzels' Bluff View.

People have a tendency to name the inanimate objects they love, and Bliss cottages are as prized by a select group of collectors in northern Michigan as a Chippendale table or an Edward Hopper painting would be to the Sotheby's crowd. The ones that have been maintained are especially valuable; in the summer of 2007, a winterized Bliss cottage on Lake Michi-gan just north of Good Hart with four bedrooms and two bathrooms was listed with Graham Real Estate for $1,295,000.

Not everyone appreciates the Bliss's early settler look, however. Mon-nie built a summer place for his longtime friend Virginia Thomas and her husband, and she was adamant that even though she wanted Monnie to build it, she didn't want "a dark old fashioned log cabin." Monnie relented and built her a more traditional cottage with wood siding and sliding glass doors.

Over the past few years the area has attracted buyers who have no ties to the history or people of the place, but just appreciate its remote beauty and "up north" status within commuting distance to the ritzy town of Har-bor Springs. Recently a young couple from Detroit bought a Bliss cottage, and after the transaction was complete, told their realtor that they only bought the place for the lake view lot it was built on. "It's a teardown," they told their real estate agent, meaning they planned to tear the cottage down and build a new and bigger and more modern summer home in its place. If the realtor could figure out a way to move the Bliss cottage he was obvi-ously so enamored with, the couple told him, he could have it for free. It would save them the expense of hiring a wrecking crew.

Local legend has it that the property on which Blisswood was built and the land further north, which was the family's original Snowberry Farm, was deeded to the Bliss family in the 1860s in lieu of payment for Almon Bliss's Civil War service. Almon was Chauncey Bliss's father, and Monnie's grandfather. Monnie's given name is Chauncey A. Bliss, the *A* standing for "Almon." According to Bonnie, the nickname "Monnie" is an auditory combination of Chauncey and Almon and was given to him for convenience so as not to be confused with his father, who went by his given name of Chauncey.

Almon moved his family to the area to farm when Chauncey was just eleven. Why else but the gift of free land from the government, Bonnie wonders good-naturedly, would the family move to northern Michigan and try to chop out a living from the forest when they had a perfectly good farm in Iowa?

Free land would have been a powerful incentive, and there is some precedent in the area for this theory; that is the way many of the first white residents of the nearby town of Bliss, settled by a distant relative of Almon, received much of their land.

By the 1930s, though, the Bliss family began evolving from farmers into developers when they built Blisswood, a resort that catered mainly to people of a certain ilk, escaping the Detroit area for a few weeks every summer. One of their first buildings was the Wigwam restaurant, followed by a few cabins, and then the bigger buildings, mainly the Krude Kraft Lodge. The Bliss family ran the restaurant, operated a gift store, took in laundry, delivered ice, decorated the tables and the cottages with fresh flowers, provided the firewood, and even helped schedule entertainment and activities. They built cabins, sold them, and rented them out. Monnie and his father had their own sawmill, a blacksmith shop, a planing shop, and an all-purpose workshop on their own property.

In the early years, the 1930s and 1940s, they logged their own woods for the lumber to build the cottages. In later years, they purchased the logs but continued to mill them in their own sawmill. All the black wrought iron hinges, door latches, and other hardware that help make the cottages so distinctive were forged in their blacksmith shop. The care they put into the buildings equaled the care they took of their lodgers. Their loyal customers appreciated a few weeks of the easy life in the north, and came back year after year, bringing their friends and relatives with them.

They were people like Maree Baxter, who, with her husband and two daughters, spent a precious three weeks down the bluff from Blisswood every summer from 1930 through 1950, renting a Bliss-built cottage, either

The Pebble or Timber Bend. When vacation time came, so anxious were they to leave Detroit behind and make the most of every moment they had in Good Hart, they would get up at three or four in the morning to arrive at Blisswood by midday.

"The cabin is so lovely," Maree wrote in her diary on Monday, August 22, 1932. "Additions this year are the two new porches, one screened and one open and the spring water piped into the kitchen and a new hanging lamp over the breakfast table and a perfectly beautiful new table and benches in the living room. Such a cozy place I never saw!"

Maree kept a diary from the time she was twelve years old until shortly before her death at sixty-four, and her Good Hart entries have been lovingly compiled into a single narrative by her grandson, Fred Cunningham, and given as gifts to a few present residents of Blisswood.

"Today is our twenty-first day at . . . The Pebble this year," she wrote on September 10, 1932. "Doesn't seem as though we could possibly have been here that long. I don't want to go back to Detroit." Then, on the next afternoon: "Weather so perfect today. Seems as though I just could not go home tomorrow. Packed all morning almost in tears."

The solution for that dreaded feeling of homesickness, not for a far-off place but for the place that you are about to leave, is simple: just don't go at all. That's what Linda Bolton does. Mostly. When she married her husband, Rick Bolton, a Dearborn attorney, he already owned a Bliss cottage on Lamkin Drive. She fell in love with him first, then with the cottage, and once she spent some time in Good Hart, she didn't want to leave, either.

"Sometimes, it's not just that I don't want to leave, but I almost feel like I can't," Linda says. "Like I'm physically unable to pack up and drive away from this place. I'm held here by magic or a spell or something. But whatever it is, it's good magic!"

Linda enjoys pointing out the distinctive features Monnie put into all the Bliss cottages: a heart-shaped rock in the center of the fireplace's dramatic stonework; lofts instead of individual bedrooms upstairs because they both encouraged family camaraderie and were easy to heat; firewood storage boxes built into the wall next to each fireplace that could be opened from the outside and the inside, picture windows on the lakeside and the driveway side of the cottages; a rare "pudding stone" somewhere visible in the exterior foundation. Near the front door, there is a small wooden box with a little door hanging on the wall. Open the door and there is a notepad and a pencil inside. Leave a note and a little red wooden flag pops up when the door is closed, so that those returning home will see that they have had a visitor.

"Everything he did, every little added detail, was to make it feel like home," Linda said.

There's almost seventy years between her experience and Maree Baxter's, but their feelings about the area appear to be much the same. The dunes and the wind off the water and the fir trees together generate an almost magical curative effect on the inhabitants here, gently pressing in a collective sense of calm. Which, beyond any hard evidence, gossip, or circumstances, is the real reason, some locals say, that no one from Good Hart could have committed the terrible crime. The woods, the lake, the ferns, and the sand simply wouldn't allow it.

On the wall that faces the Bolton's living room is a black-and-white photograph of Monnie. He is a big, lanky man, and his large frame is bent into the stern seat of a canoe. It is a sunny but cold fall day on Little Traverse Bay, and though there are no mountains within hundreds of miles of where the photo was taken, he looks like a mountain man. On his feet are a pair of knee-high suede boots, laced up in a crisscross style, the eyelets reinforced with metal studs. He is grinning.

"The summer seemed pretty short, didn't it?" Monnie wrote in the October 1959 issue of the *Driftwood Journal*. "We didn't do half the things we had planned. Next year we won't plan too much, so we won't feel guilty when we take off a day to go fishing."

Diarist Maree Baxter sums up the feeling that Monnie and the rest of the Bliss family helped create, and that spread from Blisswood to the surrounding area, decades before the Robisons ever thought of vacationing here: "We drove along the beautiful Shore Drive and took it all in again so as long as we live we can close our eyes and see it again. I shall never forget it. We have been lucky to have had that beautiful vacation spot for 24 years and we appreciate it. Never have I known the contentment that I have known in that place."

A tourist brochure circa 1955 touts the resort's charms: "Come to Blisswood this summer if you enjoy a beautiful setting, richly endowed by nature, a rare view of Lake Michigan with its interesting islands and lighthouses, lovely woodland trails, water, woods, meadow birds and wild flowers. After a gorgeous sunset view from the lookout, the flying squirrels will entertain you, as they glide from tree to tree in accompaniment to talks exchanged of the folklore of this section, which is noted for its historic interest." Those words were written by May Bliss, Chauncey's wife, Monnie's mother, and gentle hostess of Blisswood.

Those sunsets, birdsongs, the historic interest, and Maree Baxter's contentment now go for $10,000 a week in peak season. After local builder Bill Glass worked for three years to restore each cabin and all of the outbuildings, in the 1990s, Blisswood was sold to a real estate management firm based in Chicago, and then to a beer distributor in St. Louis. Glass had worked with Monnie, and though he was already a skilled builder, learned his particular style.

For a few years the place has been marketed on the Internet as a corporate retreat or family compound, the entire facility available at the weekly price of $10,000. It is that rare and exclusive combination of woodsy and elegant, and the buildings within the resort are pristine.

"Its historical significance, abundant natural resources, stunning beauty and wonderful views can only be preserved, but not replicated," reads the marketing copy on the resort's Web site.

2007

> Storytellers help a people to see and
> remember their true nature. We Indians
> have always believed one must know
> where he has been before he can know
> who he is and where he is going.
>
> —Bill Dunlop, *The Indians of Hungry Hollow*

If you can find Good Hart, then you can find Lamkin Drive. It's the first left after the tiny business district, and though it looks like it just runs down a shrub- and pine-covered dune and into the deeper woods, there are any number of notable destinations along this out-of-the-way road. St. Ignatius Church, its Native American cemetery, and the neighboring, township-owned "Church Beach" are the most public of these. Chingwa is here, too, a historic Odawa cabin built by an Odawa family of the same name, probably just after the turn of the century. It is one of just two of the area's few remaining traditionally built Odawa cabins. Look closely and you can also see the remnants of the once-gracious Lamkin Lodge that burned down in the 1940s. There are a handful of the signature Bliss-built cabins here too, scattered in the woods among the newer and oversized Cape Cods and Swiss chalets.

Still, if you are looking for a certain address, your navigational work isn't complete simply because you have found the correct road. Lamkin Drive proceeds sharply down the hill; the freshly applied asphalt ends at the bottom and things get a bit dicey from there for anyone unfamiliar with the area. The road splits into a dirt fork; to the left is South Lamkin Drive, and to the right is North Lamkin Drive. Sounds logical enough, though roads, like much else in Good Hart, aren't quite so easily read. As one longtime resident put it, "Pay no attention to the house numbers. They make no sense whatsoever, and if you try to use them to find your way, you'll just end up looking for a place to turn around."

That is one of the reasons most residents here hang a plaque at the end of their driveways with their own name or that of their cottage carved or printed on it. On any one of the Great Lakes in the summertime, "cottage" becomes just another word for "company," and polite hosts in remote areas like this make sure that they can be found by their guests.

If you are a college-educated woman older than forty and younger than ninety who summers in Good Hart, chances are good that, first, you can navigate the washboards and dust of Lamkin Drive with just an index finger on the steering wheel, and second, you are one of the Literary Ladies of Lamkin. That's the pet name Trina Hayes uses for the book club she started here six years ago. She and her husband, Larry, needed a retreat from Chicago, where Trina worked in libraries and Larry was an attorney.

In 1977 the couple found out quite by accident that a friend's mother had a log cabin, a Bliss cottage, for rent in Good Hart. They took it for the summer and every summer after that for the next thirteen years, the area affecting them much the way it did Maree and Fred Baxter decades earlier. Today, the Hayeses have their own summer home on the paved portion of Lamkin Drive, with a screened-in porch, a good breeze, and that eternally hypnotic view of Little Traverse Bay.

Trina's idea for a book club grew out of the Good Hart Property Owner's Association, which she was an active member of, but it had become bogged down with infighting and gossip. Suggestions were made for other special-interest groups—bridge, golf, tennis, and sailing clubs were all proposed, but Trina's idea for the book club was the one that took.

"Some laughed and said no one would want to talk about a book in the summer when they could be out on the beach," Trina said. "Once I had Sally Lamkin and a few other retired teachers and some of my friends, though, I knew we'd be okay."

"Okay" is a bit of an understatement. The population of the entirety of Readmond Township is less than five hundred souls, according to the U.S. Census. Perhaps fewer than half that number live in Good Hart. Halve that number again for gender and then again for adults versus children, and, using what is a very unscientific method, you get approximately sixty women in the entire township eligible for Literary Ladies of Lamkin membership in any given month. Make allowances for cancellations caused by company that lingered past the weekend, a summer cold or other ailment, or the doctor's appointment, and the eligibility field drops to forty or fifty. At a recent meeting where *The Indians of Hungry Hollow,* by Bill Dunlop, and *Digging to America,* by Anne Tyler, were discussed, thirty-two members arrived promptly at 1:00 p.m. The hostess had seats for them all.

Though the agreed-on public name for the discussion group is simply the Good Hart Book Club, Trina gets a kick out of her nickname for the group.

"Officially, you don't have to be a lady or live on Lamkin Drive to be a member, but it helps!" she joked. "I don't know what we'd do if a man wanted to join. So far, we haven't had to wrestle with that. I guess if he were secure enough to be known as a Literary Lady, then we just might welcome him in."

The Literary Ladies meet in one of the members' homes at the calculated hour of 1:00 p.m. on the third Monday of the month in June, July, and August. Food, even a light snack, is against the rules. "It's a slippery slope," Trina tells the other women, reiterating the reason for the no-food policy. "First hors d'oeuvres and the next thing you know, we're having lunch. Then it's not a book club anymore, it's a lunch club."

Members take fifteen minutes to help themselves to a beverage—usually iced tea, lemonade, or water—and then find a seat. Before the members have arrived, the hostess has already set out chairs and arranged her living room couches and loveseats in a semicircle with ample seating for all the expected attendees. In the center of this arrangement is a seat for Trina.

Setting all this up is no small task. It is not every book club whose members own summer cottages that will hold thirty women comfortably in their living rooms, though Trina insists this is not a club based on exclusivity.

The first members were invited in 2001 via a public notice posted where any public notice is posted in Good Hart if the person posting it wants any response—outside the Good Hart General Store. Today, newcomers to the area are welcome to join. When someone new moves in, she is contacted by a member of the book club and given a list of the books to be discussed and directions to each of the meeting places for that summer.

By twenty minutes after one or so, Trina opens the meeting with a call for anyone with topical announcements. Any progress on collecting recipes for the cookbook? Is the volunteer fire department still the intended beneficiary of this fund-raiser? Does everyone know that Myrt Johnson, who is nearing her hundredth birthday, will be discussing her childhood at tea on Wednesday?

Next, Trina gives a brief biography of the author whose book is to be discussed, and then she begins the formal portion of the meeting by asking the club that most simple and yet complex of literary questions: "What is this book about?"

Though everyone in the room is aware of the unsolved and now infamous murder that happened some forty years ago in their own town just north of Lamkin Drive, no one speaks of it nor of any other gossip, rumor, bad news, or even impending inclement weather. This is a book group, and they follow their library-trained leader and stay decidedly on topic. Still, many of the women have some tie, by biology or geography, to the crime.

There is Sally Kelsey, in jeans and a coral-colored woven jacket, whose own Bliss-built cottage is just two doors down from the empty lot where the Robison cottage once stood. Her sister-in-law, Linda Little, wearing bright green, sits in the next row. With her husband Bill, Sally's brother, Linda spends her summers up high on a dune in Blisswood. From her back window, her spectacular view of Little Traverse Bay angles just above the murder site. The Littles knew the Robison family well, living nearby them both in Good Hart and, coincidently, in their year-round home in the same neighborhood in Lathrup Village.

Bonnie Bliss Weitzel, daughter of Monnie and Dorothy Bliss, sporting glasses, a short haircut, and a smile, sits next to Sally. A couple chairs down is Linda Bolton, relative newcomer to Good Hart, one of the younger members at just fifty, and owner of a Bliss cottage that she and her husband have had painstakingly remodeled with the help of Monnie Bliss's long-time apprentice, Bill Glass. Bill Glass's sister-in-law Susan is here too, along with Stephanie Guyor, caretaker of St. Ignatius Church, wearing studded capri jeans and summer sandals.

"This book is about belonging somewhere," a member named Patricia Clark volunteers, breaking the ice by discussing Tyler's novel. Patricia is heading up the cookbook fund-raising project. "I just have to say right up front that I didn't care for it. It was too mundane. Nothing really happened."

"I know," said Nancy Sankaran, a redhead wearing a necklace of marble-sized silver balls. "All this hand-wringing and obsessing. I kept wanting her to get on with it."

By the close of discussion at three o'clock, it is obvious that a good number of the other members agreed with her. The quiet, behind-the-scenes finagling of husbands and wives, mothers and daughters, parents and children wasn't enough, in this book anyway, to entertain the women of Lamkin Drive. It wasn't realistic, they said, and the ending was unsatisfying.

Next summer, Trina volunteers by way of encouragement, one of the books they will be discussing is Jim Fergus's *One Thousand White Women*. Insane asylum escapes, Native American weddings, illicit love affairs, pioneer women, and horseback adventures .

"Now that's more like it!" says Nancy on her way out.

The women head home to their families and their summer lives. There is no feeling of entitlement in this room, nor any of the snootiness so easily assigned to those fortunate enough to spend uninterrupted time in a place so surrounded by physical beauty. There is only friendliness and contentment.

It is easy to imagine Shirley Robison as a member of this club. With her naturally gracious manner that so many commented on, her innate way of making people feel welcome and at ease, she would have been the perfect book club hostess. Shirley would have been the right age, the right social background, and in possession of the right economic good fortune to be able to spend the summer months in the area. Her best friend, Margaret Smith, told police that Shirley did not gossip, about others or about her own problems, which would have suited Trina Hayes just fine.

According to her mother, Shirley was an immaculate housekeeper, keeping even the clothes inside her family's dresser drawers folded neatly and perfectly aligned. She took the same care with her appearance.

"She was very meticulous about herself," said Walter Muellenhagen, Dick's business associate. "She always looked, every time you'd see her, as if she'd spent the last hour just getting every hair in place. It didn't look unnatural; it looked natural for her."

Shirley kept Summerset just as neat. "I thought for a family that was spending the summer up north that you'd see something lying around: a sand pail, a lawn chair, or a beach toy or something like that," said a happenstance visitor. "Everything was quite well picked up and everything in its place, but then they lived that way in Lathrup. Their house and their grounds were always well picked up and tidy."

Shirley was also one of those women who enjoyed the company of other women, even if she did keep her private life private. She knew how to be a girlfriend, and she put that knowledge to good use. If Shirley knew you were sick, she would call and find out if you needed anything. If you were a new mother, she would call and ask if you needed anything for the baby. More than anything though, she knew how to entertain.

"The thing that struck me most about her was at this Christmas luncheon that I went to over there," Ruth Graham told a reporter. "The fireplace in the living room was banked, completely banked, with single, potted poinsettias. One poinsettia to a pot. It made a beautiful arrangement for Christmas decorations. We had lunch, and as everybody was leaving after the luncheon, she gave each lady one of these pots to take home and keep. And I thought, 'Well isn't this a very lovely thing to do?'"

The Literary Ladies of Lamkin would have embraced Shirley, whether she would have preferred the understated family dramas or the western adventure stories or something else all together. She would have been welcome.

A Healing

I couldn't wait to grow up and move
to the city! Then, when I went away
to college, I was surprised to find
that I missed the lake. You don't
think of that when you're next to it
all the time.

—Bonnie Bliss Weitzel, Monnie's daughter, who retired
back to Good Hart

The first three weeks of July 1968 had been torturous for Aileen Fulton. Her brother had suffered a painful death from cancer on July 7, and she could not get in touch with her daughter, Shirley, or, for that matter, any of the Robisons. The night before Shirley and Dick and the kids had left to spend the summer at the cottage, Shirley had invited her mother to go along, but Aileen declined. The last time she had spoken with her daughter was on Sunday, the twenty-third of June.

After her brother died, Aileen called up to Summerset several times, day and night, for the next two weeks. She wanted to hear the comforting voice of her daughter. The operator put her calls through, but there was no answer. She tried calling Elaine, Dick's sister, and she tried calling Monnie Bliss.

"I was worrying myself sick. I was imagining everything then, all kinds of things like they might have been gassed, the furnace might have been on the blink or something in their sleep, or maybe there was a plane crash, 'cause like I said, she was the type to keep in touch with me all the time about different things, and we were very close. She was the only daughter I had."

Finally, she called Joe Scolaro and he told her not to worry, everything was fine, the family was on a trip and would be back around July 20. But of course, everything wasn't fine, and the news came on the morning of July 26, when Aileen heard her neighbor calling to her, urgently, through her open kitchen window.

"Come over here and have a cup of coffee with me!"

Aileen thought that offer rather unusual and went to the window, answering that she had already had her coffee for the day.

"Well, come on over anyway!"

Being a good neighbor, Aileen did, and in a few minutes her son Marvin and his wife, Barbara, showed up and broke the news.

"You don't have to tell me about it, I know. Something's happened to the whole family."

Between three weeks of anxiety and the vivid dream she had the week before, Shirley's mother knew her daughter was dead, even if she hadn't yet admitted it to herself. Aileen's husband, Shirley's father, had died three years before, and in her recent dream he and the Robison family were together. People might not believe in the dreams of old people, Aileen said, but that was neither here nor there. Her dream was real, and it didn't matter whether anyone believed her or not.

> I dreamt that my dead husband was in the back bedroom, laughing and talking, and Shirley and Richard's whole family was in that bedroom, but they wouldn't let me come in there. I was standing in the hallway, and they're all laughing and talking and giggling. I started telling people about this dream and they said, "Oh dreams are dreams and that's all." I figured I had worried so much about it that it was just a dream, you know? It was just that they were all standing in the room laughing and talking . . . and I can almost picture everyone, but they wouldn't let me come into the room, and I stood in the hallway.

It wasn't a dream exactly, but something like a vibration, and it seems to have temporarily inhabited another woman, whose own ethereal powers were brought to bear on the crime many months later. In August 1969, when they had begun to exhaust all the initial and obvious routes of investigation, Sheriff Zink and Undersheriff Fosmore brought a local woman, a girl, really, and a "mystic," to Summerset. Reporter Bob Clock was invited to accompany the odd little group.

B. Anne Gehman was born in Petoskey, the youngest of eight children, into a Mennonite and Amish family. When she was twelve years old, the family moved to Florida so that Anne's father could find year-round work as a surveyor. Such a large family required a year-round income to sustain, something northern Michigan had not provided. It took three years for all ten family members to make their way south, and in subsequent years Anne continued to return to northern Michigan for summer visits with relatives.

Today Gehman lives with her husband, a former Jesuit priest, outside Langley, Virginia, so she can be close to most of her current clients, who are primarily members of Congress and government officials. She stops short of actually mentioning the FBI and is irritated that her work with former First Lady Nancy Reagan has been made public on the Internet. "I don't know how that ever got out. I protect the privacy of my clients and I don't feel comfortable talking about it."

From the time she was very young, though, Gehman was aware of her psychic and spiritual skills. Her inclination has always been to use them to help people, first her immediate family, later neighbors, and finally the public.

"I started my first public work when I was young—just 15," Gehman says. "I started out helping to find people who had gone missing. Lost children usually, and sometimes even pets."

In 1968 she helped find Jean Yeaggers, a missing Florida teen. Police gave her a cigarette lighter to hold to see if she could divine any conclusions. She handled the lighter for a few minutes and soon "received images that gave me a pretty good idea of what happened." The resulting media attention made Gehman an instant celebrity in some circles, and garnered her an official invitation to consider the Robison case the next time she was in northern Michigan.

According to Clock, when she visited the site, Gehman "walked about the grounds attempting to generate so-called 'vibrations.'" At the end of her excursion she reported "that a riding stable, a church and yacht harbor are involved in the murders." Later the three men brought Gehman to Monnie Bliss's house and waited for him to come out into the front yard. They wanted to see if the mystic would receive any "vibrations" from him. She said she felt nothing.

Today, Gehman vaguely remembers the case. When asked if she has any further images that would unveil the identity of the murderer or the motive for the crime, she is silent for several minutes.

"That was so very long ago. All I can get is the money. It had something to do with the father's business and with his money. I'm afraid that's all I can do."

Up the hill from the site where her father built the Robisons a cottage, where she played as a child, where B. Anne Gehman walked, and where Aileen Fulton was on the other end of an eerily unanswered but endlessly ringing telephone, another woman has been touched by the case, too.

The fortuitously named Bonnie Bliss is the oldest of Monnie and Dorothy's three children and she is happy that she and her husband have retired to Blisswood. Bonnie grew up here, watching her father plane logs and helping her mother serve chicken dinners to resort guests at the Wigwam Restaurant in the evening and selling Odawa-made trinkets in the gift shop in the afternoon. She washed the resort's endless laundry baskets of sheets and towels and blankets with a wringer washer and listened to the explosions from the woods as her dad dispatched stubborn tree stumps. She helped her grandfather Chauncey care for his gladiolas and arranged bouquets in the cottages for visiting guests. In a word, she worked.

"I couldn't wait to grow up and move to the city!" she laughs. "Then, when I went away to college, I was surprised to find that I missed the lake. You don't think of that, when you're next to it all the time. Then suddenly, it was gone."

Bonnie's mother and father were the kind of people that northern Michigan is proud of producing, even if today their sort has grown increasingly rare. They were resourceful, tough, and happy. Pioneers when pioneering had long gone out of fashion in the rest of the state.

Bonnie's mother Dorothy was a petite redhead with a natural talent for music. She played the piano and sang so well that she could have been a professional musician. Instead, she married into a farming and woodworking family, lived in the woods, and relished her role as mother.

Bonnie's father was artistic, funny, and eccentric and knew everything about the natural world surrounding Good Hart. He didn't mind being thought of as the resort area's errand boy—as a matter of fact, he was a little proud of his ability to supply everything the township needed. Ice to keep their perishables cold, a guide to the best fishing spots, repair service for anything that was broken, and even, on the occasions that it was required, political leadership. For a dozen years, Monnie had served as township supervisor.

The only stain on her life in Good Hart is the suspicion that still comes back occasionally to remind her of the days when her father was a suspect. Her husband, Dale, has heard the whispers, though Bonnie says she has not.

"They won't say it to a direct relative," she says, showing that toughness and compassion remain in the Bliss family.

In her own way, with her own quiet strength, she has bested it. Instead of dwelling on ugly rumor, she has made Good Hart her own again. Bonnie volunteers at the Good Hart Mini Fair's bake sale every year and works at the historical museum in Cross Village. A retired pharmacist, she volunteers a couple times a month at the free clinic in Petoskey and plays host to her children, grandchildren, and their accompanying dogs as often as they will visit.

She has made a life in Good Hart in a cottage that her father and her grandfather built, a cottage across the gravel drive from the Blisswood resort and all the satisfying memories that still keep residence there. Like the one she holds onto of her father first meeting her mother, even though it happened, of course, years before she was born.

Dorothy Mange was on vacation with her parents, happy to escape an irritating boyfriend who had been in pursuit of her as a wife. She had come into marrying age and had intended to marry the boy after she returned home from a summer up north with friends. Monnie was twenty-eight years old and reaching that age when parents ask whether there will ever be a marriage. The two drove south on an errand together, and Dorothy wondered aloud how she was going to extricate herself from her engagement.

According to Bonnie, her father looked at her mother and said, "You won't have to marry him if you marry me." What happened next is a mystery, but the pair came back to Good Hart husband and wife. Bonnie laughs just thinking about the looks that must have appeared on their parents' faces when they heard the news.

"That's my favorite memory I have of my father. I've heard that story so many times that it's almost like I was there. Like it's not a story I heard someone else tell but a memory I remember."

A memory strong enough to replace anything anyone else in Good Hart thinks that they remember. Let people speculate; Bonnie is surrounded by her family, her memories, and bliss. And she has the lake again, too.

We're not likely to arrest people. Our
mission now is closure and that the
outcome is a final end.

—Sheriff Pete Wallin

Time does not heal all wounds but instead follows some to their grave. In the past four decades, Case No. 7471 has passed through the official hands of umpteen Michigan State Police detectives, three Emmet County sheriffs and four of their undersheriffs, four Sheriff's Office detectives, the State Attorney General's Office and four Emmet County prosecutors. All but one of the original law and court officers who worked the case are either retired, transferred, or dead. So are many of the other people involved, in one way or another. Chauncey Bliss is dead, and so is his son, Monnie. Few know what happened to Steve Shananaquet, though there is a rumor that he was either knifed to death or shot in a bar fight years ago.

Detectives Lloyd Stearns and John Flis are both retired, Stearns reportedly suffering from an ulcer he traces directly to the doorstep of Summerset cottage. Sheriff Zink died of cancer in December 1990 when he was only fifty-eight. His undersheriff, Clifford Fosmore, died young too, at fifty, in January 1984. Sheriff Jeffrey Bodzick, beloved in Emmet County, had even less time among the living; he died of a heart attack in July 2002 when he was only forty-eight. After his death, the county jail was rededicated in his honor and is now the more official-sounding Jeffrey P. Bodzick Office and Correctional Facility.

Despite the hoopla surrounding Emmet County Detective Bobra Johnston's announcement in 2003 of a DNA test, nothing came of it, and Johnston left the department shortly thereafter.

Sheriff Pete Wallin is the only cop left with official ties to the case—he was a gung-ho and unsullied college intern from Ferris State University's criminal justice program on random loan to Emmet County when Zink was still sheriff. Wallin, a youthful-looking and physically fit fifty-something is amused by the suggestion that the unsolved crime has put a curse on the men and women who worked it.

"It's the writers who should be worried," he laughs, sitting in his office surrounded by Mayberry and Barney Fife memorabilia. "That Petoskey reporter and that schoolteacher were writing books about this case and they both died before they finished them. And that guy from Detroit—his health isn't all that great. If I were you," Wallin winks, "I'd be thinking about *that*."

The Petoskey reporter he is referring to is Bob Clock, who covered the case from its inception for the *Petoskey News-Review.* The schoolteacher is William Grant, who moved his family away from Detroit with hopes of experiencing the good life up north. Instead, they moved into their house near Good Hart on the very day the crime was discovered. Grant taught school in Harbor Springs and was inspired enough by the case to work on his manuscript in his spare time. And "that guy from Detroit" is retired reporter Al Koski. Each of these men was or is obsessed with the case, each one using first a pencil then a typewriter then a word processor and finally a computer to try to understand, maybe for his own sanity, what happened to the Robison family. Koski has a quantity of files and research on the case that is surely awe-inspiring; Grant's files have been donated by his wife to the Harbor Springs Historical Society, temporarily stored in a local bank while the society completes its new building.

Though Sheriff Wallin oversees the investigation and takes a personal look-see at any tips that still straggle in, the actual work on the Robison case today rests within the capable and inquisitive hands of Corporal J. L. Sumpter. *J. L.* just stands for J. L., and he is as intrigued and obsessed by the case as anyone.

The obvious questions that remain are many, and retrieving the answer to any one of them would surely be germane, Sumpter says. The ones that he would most like answers to are these: Were there two shooters or just one? Where are the murder weapons? Who was Mr. Roeberts or Roberts? Did Joe Scolaro lie in his suicide note? How did Shirley Robison's luggage tag end up in the glove box of an abandoned car five years and four hundred miles later? Corporal Sumpter, the people of Good Hart, Sheriff Wallin, and unknown others would surely love to know.

There are other mysteries attached to this case that aren't quite so obvious. Mysteries that aren't necessarily part of the official record, but that vex the psyche, nonetheless. These mysteries have built over the years, transforming into myth; the more you look into them, the more convoluted and stuck the case seems.

For instance, there is the matter of Shirley Robison's assumed sexual assault. It is impossible for investigators to tell whether or not she was raped because the evidence was degraded by the time it could be collected. The obvious signs were present—her panties and girdle had been cut with something jagged and sharp, and she was naked from the waist down—but this was not proof of anything. Somehow, law enforcement officers theorize, a rape just doesn't fit in with the ambush-like nature of the crime.

Nowhere is it officially suggested that Shirley was posed to make it look like a rape, but without proof of the sexual crime, it is impossible not to consider that such an idea could have been hatched to confuse police. Or to satisfy some unfathomable need within.

A mystery, too, is Dick Robison's parentage. Years after the murder, in a casual phone call between Dick's sister, Elaine Fox, and Detective Stearns, Elaine told Lloyd that her brother was adopted by their parents as an infant, and she couldn't be absolutely certain whether or not he had known that fact before he died. Detectives checked his birth record, and found the story to be true. Ross and his first wife had adopted Dick when he was a baby. His teenaged birthmother was unmarried and financially unprepared to be a mother. Dick's adoption is a curious, though probably irrelevant matter in light of his letter to "Roebert" or "Mr. Roberts," where he addresses the man as "my father."

And then there was a rusty gun. On May 10, 2004, an old man named Leon Peter Sehoyan of Pine Street in Harbor Springs walked into the Petoskey post of the Michigan State Police, opened up a blue cloth bag, and pulled out a rusty handgun. This could be the gun that killed that family up at Good Hart, he told the desk sergeant. He didn't find the gun himself but got it from a friend. The friend, first name John, was a digger. A guy who spent his free time digging in the dirt for artifacts, old coins, lost jewelry, anything of value, even rare plants, and on one of his many sojourns found the gun buried under a rock across the road from where the Robison cottage once stood.

To everyone's surprise, John turned out to be a real person. Two months after the rusty gun was turned in to police, John Robert Peterson, who listed his address as "Phillips Cabin," was stopped in a seat belt enforcement zone, driving his multicolored "hippie" van, and told to report to the Petoskey post to relate further details of his find. He did as he was instructed, and shared with officers this story. He was driving on Shore Road north of Blisswood over Mother's Day weekend when, from his van window, he spotted an unusual wildflower. He stopped to dig it up, followed the fragile roots underneath a rock, dug deeper, and discovered the rusty gun buried there inside a partly decomposed black plastic bag.

A lab analysis suggested that the gun was a .25-caliber semiautomatic Colt 1908 Pocket Hammerless, though the firearm specialist couldn't be sure because it was so deteriorated. It was eliminated as one of the murder weapons, however, because the rifling impressions were not even close to a match. Who put the gun there, when, and why, remains yet another mystery.

A local rumor about where the actual murder weapons are hidden says that they are buried inside a grave. Depending upon whom you talk to, the gun is either buried in Island View Cemetery in the casket with Norman Bliss in Good Hart or with one of the Robison boys in Acacia Park Cemetery in Birmingham. Those who hold to this theory are adamant about it.

As proof, they point to the distasteful errand of the fall of 1968. That's when police detectives and cemetery workers gathered at Acacia Park and exhumed the bodies of Dick, Ritchie, and Gary Robison. Though the official record states it was because the coroner had missed some of the bullets in his autopsy, it makes rich material for those who are certain the police were, in reality, looking for the missing murder weapons.

Adding zest to the myth are a few idiosyncratic notes lodged deep within the Emmet County Sheriff's Office case files. The rumor about Island View Cemetery must have been given some credence, because in the 1980s a sheriff's deputy went there and found where Norman, Monnie, Chauncey, and May Bliss are all enjoying their eternal rest. The officer, making an attempt to keep his unusual work to himself, waved a metal detector over Norman Bliss's grave. The machine registered something briefly, but the deputy couldn't be sure what the item was. Visitors had entered the cemetery then, and he casually took his metal detector and left.

Sumpter says he's aware of the notes. "Curious, isn't it?" But he will say no more.

* * *

If they could, most of the Emmet County lawmen from that day would tell you, without even a bit of embarrassment, that they were and still are small-town. As boys, their path to the world cut through a woods or field, on the way to a fort or baseball diamond or boat dock; their path was never a city's cement sidewalk or back alley behind sky-blocking apartment buildings. As teenagers, they carried fishing poles and twenty-twos, not bus fare or switchblades. Still, the three men who have called themselves "sheriff" in Emmet County in the forty years since the crime have been no less driven to put it to rest with an answer and with someone in jail than any big-city cop would be. To their credit, the Detroit cops from the Michigan State Police did bring the full weight of their urban savvy and their up-to-date investigation methods down on the investigation.

"The search will continue around the clock until something concrete will develop," Undersheriff Fosmore pledged, a week after he first stepped amid the six dead and picked up the bloody hammer.

That was four decades ago. Twenty years after that, in 1988, Fosmore's boss, Richard Zink, still sheriff of Emmet County, refused to let go of the idea that the murder might yet be solved: "As long as I am sheriff the case is going to remain open."

Ten years passed and by 1988 Jeffrey Bodzick was sheriff, and he echoed Zink's pledge. By 2003 Peter A. Wallin was in office and had the benefit, or curse, of inheriting this unsolved cold case bearing thirty-five years' worth of dead-end leads, anonymous tips, a few hard facts, and countless cockamamie theories.

As Carolyn Sutherland, owner of the Good Hart General Store said, when Silent Observer offered a $2,500 reward for information leading to an arrest in the case, "I can save them the trouble—everybody's dead."

Sheriff Wallin put it a little more hopefully. "We're not likely to arrest people," he said, when his office took a fresh look at the case. "Our mission now is closure and that the outcome is a final end."

Not too many people drive down to the site of Summerset anymore. It is an empty lot with lush green grass glistening in the summer, the taller and now aging white oaks that were visible in the 1968 photographs of the cottage, and a rocky beach. If you didn't know where to look, you wouldn't be able to find it or even know that a cottage once stood here—that a family once dreamed, painted pictures, played cards, and breathed the lakeside air here.

Not too many people in Good Hart like to talk about the Robisons. What happened to them is too sad and too frightening, to remember or share with outsiders. Locals refuse to let the Robison story be the dominant one in the history of their town, and forty years later it has found its rightful place as one of the area's many legends.

The kindest way to remember the family may be the way Shirley's mother, Aileen Fulton, did, when she reimagined their afternoon visit with her, hours before they drove up to Good Hart for the last time.

All the children were there, all four of them. The two boys just got through mowing the lawns and they raked up and cleaned up the mess. They had lunch, Susan was running in and out, and Shirley and I sat and had coffee in the kitchen there. And then she said, "Mom, I've got to go home and pack . . . when I get up there, I'm just going to kick my shoes from the backdoor entrance completely across the room, and I'm going to leave them there and stretch out on the couch. I'm tired of housecleaning and of going out and of entertaining and I'm tired. I'm ready to rest."

Who's Who

Bonnie Bliss Weitzel. Daughter of Monnie Bliss, resident of Good Hart, member of the Literary Ladies of Lamkin, and present owner of a Blisswood cottage built by her father and grandfather.

Chauncey A. "Monnie" Bliss. Builder and Blisswood Resort caretaker who found the bodies of the Robison family. Son of Chauncey and May Bliss, father of Bonnie, Nancy, and Norman Bliss. Former Readmond Township supervisor who died December 27, 1980.

Chauncey P. Bliss. Founder of Blisswood Resort, an early pioneer of the Readmond Township area, husband of May Bliss, father of Monnie Bliss. Died April 23, 1978.

Dorothy E. Bliss. Wife of Monnie Bliss and mother of Bonnie Bliss Weitzel and Nancy Bliss Dickson. Died March 27, 1999.

May Bliss. Wife of Chauncey P. Bliss and mother of Monnie Bliss. Died October 6, 1982.

Norman Bliss. Teenaged son of Monnie and Dorothy Bliss who was killed in a motorbike accident between Cross Village and Good Hart on June 23, 1968.

Raymond Britt. Wealthy Ohio industrialist who married Dick Robison's former secretary, Wanda Hensley.

Wanda Hensley Britt. Dick Robison's secretary from 1963 to 1965. Later married the wealthy industrialist Raymond Britt, forty years her senior.

John Norman Collins. Eastern Michigan University student suspected by police in the Co-Ed Murders that took place in Washtenaw County between 1967 and 1969. Convicted for one of the murders in 1970, now serving a life sentence in Marquette Branch Prison.

John Flis. Detective with the Michigan State Police who investigated the Robison murders.

Harry Ford. Vice president of Delta Faucet Company and Dick Robison's contact for contracts between Delta and R. C. Robison and Associates.

Clifford Fosmore. Emmet County undersheriff in 1968, one of the first officers on the scene of the murders, and the top lawman in charge of the investigation for the first few days. His boss, Sheriff Richard Zink, was on vacation in Yellowstone National Park.

Judith Guest. Michigan native and best-selling author of *Ordinary People* who also wrote a mystery novel, *The Tarnished Eye,* inspired by the Robison case and the Co-Ed Murders.

Frank Kelley. Michigan's attorney general from 1963 to 1998 (nicknamed "Michigan's Eternal General"). Backed up Donald Noggle when he declined to swear out an arrest warrant in the case.

Aldred Koski. Newspaper reporter for Detroit area newspapers who has covered the case since 1968. He also produced a two-part radio documentary for WKNR titled *The Six Who Died,* which aired in March 1969.

Tom Mair. Childhood friend of Randy Robison, operator of the Web site www.unsolvedhomicide.com, member of Northern Michigan Crime Stoppers.

Donald Noggle. Emmet County prosecutor from 1957 to 1958 and 1969 to 1973. Declined to swear out an arrest warrant in the crime, citing lack of proof of guilt.

Richard Robison. Father of the Robison family and founder of R. C. Robison and Associates as well as publisher of the arts magazine *Impresario.* Murdered when he was forty-two.

Shirley Robison. Mother of the Robison family, stay-at-home mom, murdered when she was forty.

Ritchie Robison. Oldest son of the Robison family, graduate of Southfield High School, student at Eastern Michigan University, murdered when he was nineteen.

Gary Robison. Middle son of the Robison family, student at Southfield High School, murdered when he was seventeen.

Randy Robison. Youngest son of the Robison family, murdered when he was twelve.

Susan Robison. Youngest child of the Robison family and only daughter, murdered when she was seven.

Joseph Raymond Scolaro III. Army Security Agency veteran and employee of Dick Robison's advertising firm and arts magazine, husband to Lora Lee Scolaro, father of two sons, law enforcement's chief suspect, died by suicide March 8, 1973.

Kathleen "Kitty" Scolaro. Joseph Scolaro's mother and his secretary at Dimensional Research.

Lora Lee Scolaro. Joseph Scolaro's wife and mother to his two sons.

Lloyd Stearns. State police detective assigned to the Robison investigation.

Pete Wallin. Sheriff of Emmet County from 2002 until the present day.

Sources and Resources

Call the Law

Michigan State Police Report on Case No. 7471

Michigan State Police crime scene photographs

Fred Lovelace's photographs for the *Petoskey News-Review,* July 1968

Emmet County Sheriff's Office radio log for July 1968

Interviews with Sheriff Pete Wallin, May 31, 2007, and July 10, 2007

Paul E. Petosky, Postmarks from the Past, a regular column in the *Great Lakes Marina* newspaper and a Web site, http:postmarks/grandmaraismichigan.com

Emmet County tax certificate dated October 25, 1910

Brochure from Chippewa Cove Woods

Historical signs posted along M-119, The Tunnel of Trees

"Mystery Shrouds Area of Mass Murder since Indian Legend Days," by Bob Clock, *Petoskey News-Review,* August 1, 1968

Will Be Back

Michigan State Police Report on Case No. 7471

Michigan State Police crime scene photographs

Autopsy files of Emmet County medical examiner Dr. Richard Weber

Letter from pathologist Dr. Jean Webster to Jensen's Animal Hospital dated July 30, 1968

Emmet County medical examiner's property recovery form dated July 23, 1968

Interview with Aileen Fox by Al Koski, 1968

"Probe Emmet Mass Murder; Family of Six Found Dead at Blisswood," by Fred Lovelace, *Petoskey News-Review,* July 23, 1968

"Rule Mass Murder Premeditated," *Petoskey News-Review,* July 24, 1968

"Zink Returns to Head Robison Probe," by Bob Clock, *Petoskey News-Review,* July 26, 1968

"Slayer of 6 Hidden by Lack of Motive," *Detroit News,* August 9, 1968

"4 Bodies Exhumed in Robison Investigation," *The Eccentric,* November 1, 1968

The Boss

Michigan State Police Report on Case No. 7471

Interview with accountant Cal Mackey conducted at his office at 10½ Mile and
  Greenfield and Oak Park on November 24, 1969, by Detectives Lloyd Stearns
  and John Flis

State police interview with Richard Stockwell, former R. C. Robison and Associates employee

State police interview with Ross Robison, Dick Robison's father

State police interview with Joseph R. Scolaro III

State police interview with Pastor Harvey Peters of Calvary Lutheran Church in
  Southfield, Michigan

State police interview with Dr. Alexander Dukay of Ypsilanti State Hospital

Results of Walter Muellenhagen's polygraph test

Autopsy files of Emmet County medical examiner Dr. Richard Weber

New Catholic Dictionary

Writings of Richard Robison

Editorials published in *Impresario* Magazine

"Victims Close-Knit; Did Things Together," by Bob Clock, *Petoskey News-Review,*
  July 24, 1968

The Mentals

Michigan State Police Report on Case No. 7471

Emmet County Sheriff's Office report

Historical records of the Northern Michigan Asylum for the Insane

"Deadlier Than the Snake Pits? Reporter's 5 Days in an Asylum," by Stephen Cain,
  Detroit News, June 27, 1971

The Phony

Michigan State Police Report on Case No. 7471

Interview with accountant Cal Mackey conducted at his office at 10½ Mile and
  Greenfield and Oak Park on November 24, 1969, by Detectives Lloyd Stearns
  and John Flis

Interview with Dr. Roger Smith and Margaret Smith, friends and neighbors of the
  Robisons, by Al Koski, 1969

Interview with retired Michigan State Police detective John Flis at his home, by Al
  Koski, July 18, 1998

State police interview with Joe Scolaro

Obituary of J. Raymond Scolaro, Joe Scolaro's father

Military records of Joe Scolaro

Telephone records for Summerset, the Robisons' Good Hart cottage, and for Joe
   Scolaro's Wallace Street home in Birmingham
Financial records of R. C. Robison and Associates

Gun Country

Michigan State Police Report on Case No. 7471
Emmet County Sheriff's Office report
"Where Is the Gun That Killed the Robison Family?" by Joseph E. Wolff, *Detroit
   News*, June 27, 1971
"Problem of Ecology & Economics," by Keith Matheny, *Petoskey News-Review*, July
   1, 1997
Michigan Department of Natural Resources hunting season records
State police ballistics report on Case No. 7471
"Find 14 Spent .22 Shells in Robison Cottage Closet," *Petoskey News-Review*, Sep-
   tember 14, 1998

Following the Money

Interviews with Sheriff Pete Wallin, May 31, 2007, and July 10, 2007
Financial records of R. C. Robison and Associates
State police interview with Roger and Margaret Smith
State police interview with Detroit National Bank manager Frank Joity
Walter Muellenhagen's notes on Dick Robison's new business venture
State police interview with Ross Robison
Oakland County Probate Court records from July 1968
State police interview with accountant Cal Mackey
State police interview with New Hudson Airport managers Arnold Park and
   William McKinley
Telephone records for Dick Robison's home on Dolores Street in Lathrup Village
State police interview of Joe Scolaro
State police interview with Helen Hoeft, secretary at Delta Faucet
Records of Oakland County assistant prosecutor and forensic accountant Eugene
   Freedman
"Big Airport Deal Adds New Mystery to Robison Case," United Press Interna-
   tional, September 5, 1969
"A New, Startling Report on the Bizarre Events and Strange Dealings That Fore-
   shadowed Murder," by William Schmidt and Al Koski, *Detroit Free Press*, No-
   vember 8, 1970

The Tipsters

Michigan State Police Report on Case No. 7471

Emmet County Sheriff's Office report

Letter from Sheriff Richard Zink to Martin S. Hayden, editor of the *Detroit News*, August 7, 1968

Typed letter addressed to the Director of the Federal Bureau of Investigation, October 4, 1972

Memo from unknown state police detective to Captain Guy Babcock, September 15, 1969

Letter from an anonymous correspondent to attorney general Frank J. Kelley, July 28, 1988

State police interview with Karl Olbrich and friends

Telephone records of Joe Scolaro's Wallace Street home in Birmingham

"Reward Offered in Unsolved Mass Murder," by John Charles Robbins, *Petoskey News-Review*, June 24, 1998

"Police Ask News' Aid in Robison Murders," *Detroit News*, August 11, 1968

"Is Key to Robisons' Killer in Classified ad?" by Joseph E. Wolff, *Detroit News*, January 5, 1969

"Robison Murders Year Ago—Still No Motive," by Bob Clock, *Petoskey News-Review*, June 25, 1969

"Detroiter Confesses to Good Hart Murders—but Is Another Phony," by Bob Clock, *Petoskey News-Review*, April 24, 1969

A Leg Man

Michigan State Police Report on Case No. 7471

Emmet County Sheriff's Office file

State police interview with Wanda Hensley Britt

State police interview with Gail Cornforth Barnes

State police interview with Bonnie Jean Scrull

State police interview with Corrine Loop Newton

State police interview with Glenda Sutherland

State police interview with Leo Sawchuck

Financial records of R. C. Robison and Associates

Polygraph examination of Joe Scolaro

State police interview with Ernest Gilbert

State police interview with Richard Stockwell

Cleveland Police Department report on Raymond Britt

Palm Beach Shores Visitors and Convention Bureau

State police interview with Virgil Wheaton

"Religious Medal May Be Clue to Mass Murder Mystery Man," *Detroit News*, March 24, 1969

The Alibi

Michigan State Police Report on Case No. 7471

The Blue Book of Gun Values, 28th ed., (Blue Book Publications, 2007)

Hit Man: A Technical Manual for Independent Contractors, by Rex Feral (Boulder, CO: Paladin Press, 1983)

Two-color pamphlet advertising the AR-7 produced in the mid-1960s by the Armalite Corp.

Memo from gun expert Harold Gunder to Emmet County sheriff's detective Jerry Hartman, September 1, 1991

State police interviews with Lora Lee Scolaro

State police interview with Walter Muellenhagen

Weather report of June 25, 1968, for Southfield, Michigan, and Good Hart, Michigan

State police investigation photos of the basement of the Robison home on Dolores Street in Lathrup Village, Michigan

Financial records of R. C. Robison and Associates

State police interview with Margaret Smith

Closing In

Michigan State Police Report on Case No. 7471

Southfield, Michigan, police report of the suicide of Joe Scolaro

Michigan State Police photographs of Albert Faulman's target range on Elizabeth Lake Road outside the town of Union Lake, Michigan

Interview with Herbert Johnson by Detectives Lloyd Stearns and John Flis, November 12, 1969, at Johnson's place of work, the Utley-James Construction Company in Pontiac, Michigan

Letter from Charles Meyers, Senior Crime Laboratory Analyst, retired, to Sheriff Richard Zink, dated July 29, 1988

Michigan State Attorney General records

The Criminal Mind by Katherine Ramsland, PhD (Cincinnati, OH: Writer's Digest, 2002)

"Arrest Robison Associate over Insufficient Checks," United Press International, September 15, 1969

"Robison's Associate Charged with Fraud," *The Eccentric,* September 18, 1969

"Robison Murder Suspect Found Dead," by Jim Herman, *Detroit News,* March 9, 1973

The Case for Prosecution

Michigan State Police Report on Case No. 7471

Emmet County Sheriff's Office files

State police interviews with Joe Scolaro

Letter from Emmet County prosecutor Donald C. Noggle to Sheriff Richard Zink dated January 13, 1970

Statement from *Petoskey News-Review* reporter John R. "Bob" Clock to Sheriff Richard Zink, signed but undated

Memo from unknown State Police detective to Captain Guy Babcock dated September 15, 1969

Virginia Tech study by the Campus Alcohol Abuse Prevention Center in Blacksburg, Virginia

Al Koski interview with Bill Glass, notes dated March 3, 2000

Telephone conversation between author and Al Koski, September 16, 2007

State police interview with chief assistant Oakland County prosecutor Ronald Covault

"Harbor Youth Killed in Crash Is 3rd in Week in Emmet County," *Petoskey News-Review*, June 24, 1968

"Noggle Reviewing Robison Evidence from State Police," by Fred Lovelace, *Petoskey News-Review*, January 6, 1970

"Robison Murders Believed Solved," by Joseph E. Wolff, *Detroit News*, January 6, 1970

"Noggle Expects Robison Decision Soon," *Petoskey News-Review*, January 7, 1970

"Noggle: Not Enough Evidence for Arrest—But Robison Massacre Case Not Closed," by Fred Lovelace, *Petoskey News-Review*, January 14, 1970

The Leavenworth Letter Theory

Michigan State Police Report on Case No. 7471

Letter from Alexander Bloxom to Michigan State Police, January 12, 1970

Michigan State Police criminal history card for Alexander Bloxom, October 10, 1957

Kansas Branch of the Federal Bureau of Investigation records of an interview of Alexander Bloxom by Special Agent Jack H. Williams

State police interview with Alexander Bloxom

State police interview with Mark Warren Brock

State police interview with Robert Matthews

State police interview with Walter and Bessie Bloxom

"Retired Detective's Theory: Suicide Ended Case in 1973," by Al Koski, *Oakland Press*, July 22, 1998

Manhunts in the North Woods

"Backhoe Bandit Says He Was Attacked," by Sheri McWhirter, *Traverse City Record-Eagle*, August 8, 2007

Official request for laboratory examination from Detective Bobra Johnston to the Michigan State Police Forensic Science Division, August 1, 2002

Letters dated May 1, May 10, May 12, May 13, and May 20, 2002, from Linda Venn of Davidson, Michigan, to Emmet County law enforcement and court officials

Laboratory report from Michigan State Police forensic scientist Jeffrey Nye to Detective Bobra Johnston dated June 25, 2003

Laboratory report from Michigan State Police Firearms, Toolmarks and Explosives Sub-unit dated June 25, 2003

State of Michigan Department of Public Health report dated August 15, 1968

Interviews with Sheriff Pete Wallin, May 31, 2007, and July 10, 2007

Emmet County Sheriff's Office official Web site

Multiple news accounts of the murder of Tara Grant

Crime Lab: A Guide for Nonscientists by John Houde (Rollingbay, WA: Calico Press, 2006)

"Continue Search for Mass Slayer," by Bob Clock, *Petoskey News-Review*, July 25, 1968

"Sheriff Hopes for Closure, Finality in Baffling Murder That Shocked Area 35 Years Ago," by Al Koski, *Petoskey News-Review*, May 20, 2003

"Murder Case DNA May Not Be Usable," by Steve Zucker, *Petoskey News-Review*, May 21, 2003

The Sleuths

Michigan State Police Report on Case No. 7471

Telephone conversation between author and Al Koski, September 16, 2007

E-mail exchanges with Al Koski, August and September 2007

Interview with Judith Guest, September 12, 2007

Appearance by Judith Guest at the Lincoln, Michigan, public library, September 12, 2007

Interview with Tom Mair, June 9, 2007

Al Koski's interview with state police detective John Flis

The Michigan Murders by Edward Keyes (New York: Reader's Digest Press, 1976)

Letter from Dean R. Luedders of the Real Estate Division of the National Bank of Detroit to Undersheriff Clifford Fosmore, August 27, 1968

Letter from attorney general Frank J. Kelley and assistant attorney general Robert Ianni of the Criminal Division to post commander Lt. David Leik, August 29, 1988

State police interview with Reverend Harvey Peters

Handwritten notes from the files of the Emmet County Sheriff's Office on a sheet of paper from a yellow legal pad, dated "8–12"

Letter from Tom Mair to Aileen Fox, July 11, 1994

Letter from Aileen Fox to Detective Lloyd Stearns

"Seek Link in Robison Murders," by Jane Denison, United Press International, August 4, 1969

"Robison Massacre Site Will Be Torn Down," by Joseph E. Wolff, *Detroit News,* September 5, 1968

"To Raze Murder Cottage in Unsolved Emmet Case," by Bob Clock, *Petoskey News-Review,* February 24, 1969

"Obsession; Veteran Reporter Writing Book on Good Hart Murder Case," by Deidre Tomaszewski, *Petoskey News-Review,* October 20, 2000

"On the Trail of a Killer," by Tom Mair, *Northern Express,* August 2004

"Retired Harbor Springs Teacher Offers Opinion on Murders," by Janenne Irene Froats, *Petoskey News-Review,* July 23, 1993

"Tip Line Continues in Robison Murders," by John Charles Robbins, *Petoskey News-Review,* October 23, 1998

"Murders Became an Obsession to Reporter," by Steve Zucker, *Petoskey News-Review,* May 20, 2003

The Good People of Good Hart

"How the Retired Man May Serve His Country," by John J. Gafill, *American Forests Magazine,* June 1962

"Mystery Has Long Shrouded Good Hart Area," *Petoskey News-Review,* August 10, 1968

Personal letters of Bishop Baraga. Archives of Bishop Baraga, Diocese of Marquette, Michigan

Interview with Stephanie Guyor, October 13, 2007

Driftwood Journal by Monnie Bliss

Interview with Sheriff Pete Wallin

Interview with Virginia Taylor, August 20, 2007

A Bliss House

House tour and interview with Linda Bolton, August 19, 2007

Interview with Trina Hayes, August 19, 2007

Interview with Bonnie Bliss Weitzel, October 13, 2007

Interview with Carolyn Sutherland, June 2, 2007

Northern Michigan real estate listings

Issues of the *Driftwood Journal* by Monnie Bliss

"Fred and Maree Baxter at The Pebble and Timber Bend 1930 to 1950," a diary of Good Hart summer visitor Maree Baxter, compiled by her grandson, Fred Cunningham, May 2006

Brochure for Blisswood, 1955

Web site for Blisswood resort, www.blisswoodmichigan.com

The Literary Ladies of Lamkin

Attendance at the August 20, 2007, meeting of the Good Hart Book Club, aka
"The Literary Ladies of Lamkin"
Interview with Trina Hayes, August 19, 2007
Interview with Linda Bolton, August 19, 2007
Interview with Stephanie Guyor, October 13, 2007
Interview with Bonnie Bliss Weitzel, October 12, 2007
The Indians of Hungry Hollow by Bill Dunlop (Ann Arbor: University of Michigan
Press, 2004)
State police interview with Margaret Smith
State police interview with Walter Muellenhagen

A Healing

Interview with Bonnie Bliss Weitzel
Interview with B. Anne Gehman
Al Koski's interview with Aileen Fulton
State police interview with Aileen Fulton

Epilogue: Status of Case No. 7471

Typed note from State Trooper John Flis to Sheriff Richard Zink dated April 5, 1971
Interviews with Sheriff Pete Wallin, May 31, 2007, and July 10, 2007
Interviews with Corporal J. L. Sumpter, July 10, 2007

Further Reading

Following the completion of this book, and at the urging of Petoskey, Michigan, schoolteacher and crime researcher Richard A. Wiles, the Petoskey Public Library has established an archive of research and related materials regarding the unsolved Robison murder case. Reference librarian Drew Cherven is in charge of cataloging this collection. All of the research used by the author in writing *When Evil Came to Good Hart* can be accessed there: Petoskey Public Library, 500 East Mitchell Street, Petoskey, MI 49770.

Text design by Mary H. Sexton

Typesetting by Delmastype, Ann Arbor, Michigan

Text Font: Hoefler Text
Unlike many fonts, created over the centuries to be
cast in metal and redrawn to bring them into the digital age,
Hoefler Text was designed specifically as a digital font in 1991.
    —*courtesy* typography.com